Seem To Have Been There Before

Wanderings Around Tennessee's Cumberland Plateau

Bill Parnell

For Brody

As the twilight began to fall, I sat down on the mossy instep of a spruce. Not a bush or tree was moving; every leaf seemed hushed in brooding repose. One bird, a thrush, embroidered the silence with cheery notes, making the solitude familiar and sweet, while the solemn monotone of the stream sifting through the woods seemed like the very voice of God, humanized, terrestrialized, and entering one's heart as to a home prepared for it. Go where we will, all the world over, we seem to have been there before.

Travels in Alaska

John Muir, 1879

ACKNOWLEDGMENTS

A special thank you is owed to all of my friends that were crazy enough to follow me on these trips. I sincerely hope you never learn your lesson.

Chapter I

Most Sublime and Comprehensive Picture

"After a few miles of level ground in the luxuriant tangle of brooding vines, I began the ascent of the Cumberland Mountains, the first real mountains that my foot ever touched or eyes held. The ascent was by a nearly regular zigzag slope, mostly covered up like a tunnel by overarching oaks. But there were a few openings where the glorious forest road of Kentucky was grandly seen, stretching over hill and valley, adjusted to every slope and curve by the hands of Nature – the most sublime and comprehensive picture that ever entered my eyes. Reached the summit in six or seven hours, a strangely long period of up-grade work to one accustomed only to the hillocky levels of Wisconsin and adjacent states."

A Thousand Mile Walk to the Gulf

John Muir, 1867

"So where are you going?" That is the reaction I get from most people when I talk about going to the Plateau. This question would make sense if I was not living in West Tennessee, where nearly every longtime resident grew up either going to Gatlinburg and the Great Smoky Mountains each spring/summer/fall, attending University of Tennessee football games in Knoxville, or at minimum occasionally going to Atlanta via Interstate 24. On those travels they have all ascended and descended the Cumberland Plateau on each and every trip. How did they miss it? It isn't like they blanked out and missed the scenery. They saw the climb up the eastern or western escarpment with the roadway blasted into the cliffs sides covered in perpetual trickling springs (or ice hummocks in the winter), they felt their ears pop with the changing air pressure, they saw the rock slide nets and the runaway truck ramps, they probably strained their necks looking off the side of the road on the Tennessee Valley side, and maybe even understood that they were seeing the purple lumps of the Smoky Mountains on the eastern horizon. But they probably filed the experience under being in East Tennessee, not having understood the true nuances of the geography in

1

front of them.   Even for the people that live in the areas near the Cumberland Plateau, it is often referred to as "the mountain", even though on top it is flatter in some areas than the bottomlands of West Tennessee. Perhaps some of the disrespect comes out of simply being overshadowed by the most visited national park in the nation barely 50 miles away. Despite people's ignorance or apathy, it is still there.   On every TV weather forecast that zooms out to the graphic relief map of the Eastern U.S., the greater Appalachian Plateau stands out as clear as day. It is that rough patch of map stretching from northern Alabama to western New York, slightly distinguished from the even rougher patch of map containing the Appalachian Mountains to the east.

Geologically speaking, the greater Appalachian Plateau is a dissected plateau of the Appalachian range, which has been around for a very long time. The Appalachians were formed around 300 million years ago making them some of the oldest mountains on earth (although nowhere near the 3 billion year old ranges in Africa). They stood as tall as the Alps before the long effects of erosion.   Fossils that are 450 million years old have been found in the limestone of Cades Cove. To give you some perspective in all of this, the Rockies are 80 million years old. The Himalayas are 50 million years old (and still growing!). What about that great back drop for all your favorite episodes of Grey's Anatomy and Frasier? Mount Rainier is a baby, just 500,000 years old. And that condo on that golf resort on Hilton Head that your stuck up neighbor talks about non-stop? It's sitting on land that is barely 5,000 years old. Just waiting on one big wave!

Of course, you probably haven't heard of the greater Appalachian Plateau because nobody actually refers to it that way. In its northern parts it is called the Allegheny Plateau and the Allegheny Mountains.   In its southern section it is the Cumberland Mountains and the Cumberland Plateau, which is especially marked in Tennessee with the wide smooth valley on its eastern side, separating it from the Appalachians. Tennessee's piece is approximately 55 miles wide on the northern border with Kentucky and 40 miles wide on the Alabama and Georgia border. It averages between 1,700 and 1,900 feet above sea level, with some of the Cumberland Mountains in the northern section reaching 3,000 feet. While there are some prominent mountain ridges, the typical topographical features, past the sharp eastern and western escarpments, are rolling hills that are occasionally interrupted with steep gorges up to 1,000 feet deep. These gorges are still being carved by streams and rivers fighting their way toward some piece of the Tennessee or Cumberland Rivers, forging a rugged wonderland of waterfalls and caves under open sandstone bluff overlooks along their way. Most of the millions of travelers in the millions of cars passing along Interstate 40 and Interstate 24 barely give it a passing thought.

The Cumberland Plateau has not always been so ignored. The Shawnee and Cherokee tribes never established permanent settlements there, but they did use the area as a seasonal hunting ground and took advantage of the rock houses and caves in the gorges for temporary shelter. Daniel Boone and the longhunter pioneers did the same on their journey through. When James Robertson first led settlers into the Tennessee Valley in 1776, the seamless 1,000 foot wall of stone stopped them in their tracks. After crossing the rugged southern Appalachians, they had no idea how to get past the Plateau. So Colonel John Donelson co-founded Nashville by floating down the Tennessee River to the Ohio River, going up stream on the Ohio River to the Cumberland River, and then going up stream on the Cumberland River to settle Middle Tennessee, effectively making a 1,000 mile long gigantic circle.

In 1863, after the losing the Battle of Stones River, Confederate General Braxton Bragg ultimately took the Army of Tennessee up the Plateau to escape the advancing Union Army. It seemed like a good place to hide and it worked for a while. Of course he probably should have stayed up there. Bragg later tried to occupy Chattanooga, then got kicked out. He had a victory at the Battle of Chickamauga but his luck didn't last. Grant, Sherman, and Hooker routed him off Lookout Mountain and Missionary Ridge, which opened the door for Sherman's march to the sea. Bragg was called to Richmond and lost his job.

On September 10, 1867, a young Scottish immigrant from Indiana who had recently recovered from a mill accident that almost blinded him, beheld a mountain for the first time in his life and spent the next few weeks traveling south through Tennessee along the ridges of the Plateau. Upon recovering his sight, John Muir had decided to dedicate his life to studying the natural world. He intended to walk to the Gulf of Mexico, travel to South America, climb the Andes to find the head waters of the Amazon, build a raft, and float to the Atlantic Ocean. First he climbed the Cumberland Plateau. Fortunately for all of humanity, his wild plan ended with malaria in Florida. After he recovered he decided to set out for "healthy California", and he ended up in the Yosemite Valley. It was here where he became an ardent environmental evangelist, founding the Sierra Club and petitioning Congress to establish National Parks. His name is all over glaciers, trails, mountains, and monuments dedicated to the preservation of our natural world. He even has his own official holiday, John Muir Day, celebrated on April 21st from California to Scotland. His books are part travel literature, part poetry, part spiritual testimony, and were a significant influence on my attempt at writing this book.

In the first half of the 20th century, the Plateau experienced booms and busts in timber and coal. The coal was quickly depleted and old growth hardwoods were clear cut. By the second half of the 20th century, the Plateau remained one the most sparsely populated areas in Tennessee, but with a scarred up landscaped of depleted resources. If you know much about the history of land conservation in the Eastern U.S., those are the necessary conditions to get areas protected, and so the parks began to be established. Today, the Plateau contains the greatest concentration of protected land in Tennessee (outside of the Appalachians along the far eastern edge of the State).

However; I didn't come to my adventures on the Plateau by watching weather forecast maps, trying to settle Middle Tennessee, running from the Union Army, or trying to travel to South America. I passed over it with ignorance and apathy for a long time too. Even after I first started planning my day hiking and backpacking adventures, they were all in the Great Smoky Mountains National Park. But sometime after beginning my post college career, vacation days became rarer and my free time became scarcer. I started to look for places with a little less travel time than the five hours of driving and hour time zone loss that I experienced on the Smokies trips. There have been many mornings I have left my home in Jackson at sunrise to drive to the National Park and between picking people up, fighting tourist traffic, getting permits, and dropping off cars (if we weren't doing a loop), we found ourselves at the trailhead starting to race the sun disappearing over the high ridges and setting up our first camp in the dark after only two or three miles of trail behind us. I began to hope that there were some closer mountain adventures that I had overlooked.

In the summer of 2002, once again it was time to plan a trip. I often begin to plot my trips not by doing Google searches on "best hikes", but actually by looking at road maps. On every map there are these wonderful green blobs that come in all sizes and permutations. There are all types; state parks, national parks, wildlife refuges, national forests, state forests, wild and scenic rivers, national monuments, federally designated wilderness areas, etc. If a green blob piques my interest, then I start researching it for possibilities. While I was planning for that particular summer trip I noticed the amount of green blobs that we were blowing past on our way to the Smokies. So I ended up picking the most familiar place to me at the time, which was Fall Creek Falls State Park. While that particular backpacking trip did not turn out as well as I expected it to, it started a long journey that has led me to tromp all over the varying corners of the Plateau while giving me a few good stories along the way. Over the course of these trips, the Plateau has become a place that will quickly provide as much adventure as I am willing to put in effort. With just a little bit of this effort, the reward is quickly attained. On most trips I may get on the road as the sun is rising, but I find myself eating lunch on a boulder on a sunny cliff top, watching hawks circle in the gorge below. Over these years it has become a familiar place to me, never failing to give what I am seeking. I am always ready to go back as quickly as I can.

The primary sources for the stories in this book were readily available. From the time I was 13 years old, I have kept some kind of notes or journals of my outdoor adventures. These chapters were written by going back to my old journals on each area and trying to describe what I have seen and done. I have also made an attempt at some mild history and conservation lessons. Don't worry, I have made them as painless as possible.

Ultimately this book is meant to share these stories in a way that will hopefully be at least slightly entertaining, but even if found boring will contain enough information to serve as a guide if one were attempting to replicate any of the trips. Descriptions of difficulty are based on hiking trails in the Eastern U.S. and nothing requires skills beyond putting one foot in front of the other (or holding a canoe paddle). I have also tried to provide the best maps possible to explain the stories and tried to be true to mileage estimates and elevation changes (although for the trips outside the nice maps of official State Park boundaries, I would suggest looking at multiple sources before you attempt them). The maps included in this book are meant to help you understand the narrative. Before actually going into the wild, get a real map. See the Notes Section for details about my sources and places to find useful information.

Of course I hope I have also added enough to the stories, beyond just the hard facts, to actually inspire some new adventures. There are plenty to be had out there. If there is one thing I have learned in my wilderness travels, there really is no telling what is waiting just over the hilltop. And the only way to find out, is to go out.

Chapter II

Frozen Head State Park

I don't want to think about how many times I drove past the exit to Frozen Head before my first visit. With 24,000 acres, it is the second to largest park (considering contiguous acres) on the Plateau, only slightly smaller than Fall Creek Falls. This park is truly in the edge of the Cumberland Mountains region, where the Plateau loses much of its flat top and starts to roll out into small peaks and valleys. Unlike most of the other places on the Plateau that I discuss in this book, the main attractions here are the summits, not gorges and waterfalls. The high point in the park is Frozen Head Mountain, with an elevation of 3,324 feet, but there are 13 other peaks over 3,000 feet, which enable plenty of good overlooks into the Tennessee Valley and to the Great Smoky Mountains on the horizon. There are over 50 miles of trail here and many back country campsites, which make for a lot of good backpacking trip possibilities.

In reality the reason why I waited so long to visit Frozen Head was because it is in the very northeastern part of the Plateau. From my home in West Tennessee, I could almost be at the edge of the Great Smoky Mountains National Park in about the same drive time. Now that I have visited the park, I know that the distance is a very poor excuse. This place would be worth going to no matter where it was located. It has many of the same features as the Smokies, but in a more compact package and with a lot less crowds.

Access is relatively easy. From I-40, take exit 347, and follow Highway 27 going north to Harriman. Follow Highway 27 through Harriman and go to Wartburg, then turn right (east) on to Highway 62. After 2 miles on Highway 62, turn on to Flat Fork Road. The park entrance is 4 miles down Flat Fork Road.

The conservation history of this place is a little more unique than other parts of the Plateau. A large tract was purchased by the State in 1894 as a site for what became Brushy Mountain State Prison. There was an idea to use prison labor to mine coal in the area, which never turned into a large operation. Old evidence from mining is scattered throughout the park and

7

mining activity in the area continued into the 1970's. For one reason or another, Brushy Mountain Prison became quite a cultural icon until it was finally closed in 2009. The most famous inmate was James Earl Ray, who assassinated Martin Luther King, Jr. But the name, "Brushy Mountain Prison", seemed to capture people's imaginations, and the prison is featured in Country songs (my favorite being *Brushy Mountain Conjugal Trailer* by Old Crow Medicine Show), novels by John Grisham and Cormac McCarthy, and was even the "final destination" for Hannibal Lecter in *The Silence of the Lambs.*

The remainder of the forest followed the more typical pattern of history. Of course commercial logging operations cut most of the timber by the end of the 1920's. In 1933 Morgan State Forest was created using a large tract of the prison land. In 1970 the park was officially established, and in 1988 all but 330 acres were declared a State Natural Area.

But most recently, this park has received notoriety as the location of the Barkley Marathons. This ridiculously difficult ultramarathon was first run in 1986 and existed in relative obscurity for decades, only rarely being reported on in runner specific publications and discussed by word of mouth/internet in ultra runner forums. In 2012, a documentary was filmed on the race titled *The Barkley Marathons: The Race That Eats Its Young.* A few years later that documentary found its way to the Netflix library and social media locked in on it. International fame has ensued.

The history of the race is also linked to Brushy Mountain Prison. In 1977, James Earl Ray escaped from Brushy Mountain and a highly televised man hunt followed. He was captured 55 hours later after only covering 8 miles through the rugged Cumberland Mountains. The founder of the Barkley Marathons, Gary "Lazarus Lake" Cantrell, joked that he could have gone 100 miles in the same amount of time, and hence the idea for the race was born. It is a 60 hour race with 5 loops that are claimed to be 20 miles long. Of course the route is different every year, and the mileage is always represented to be 20.0 miles. Most that have studied it with GPS and satellite maps claim the loops are closer to 26 miles. In any event, no one really knows what the course is going to be other than Lazarus. There were no finishers until 1995 and no more until 2001. As of the 2017 race, there have only been 18 finishes by 15 runners.

After watching the documentary on Netflix, I decided to make the race my inspiration for my first experience in the park. Instead of backpacking, I decided to explore the park by trail running as much of it as possible over two days. In keeping with the spirit of the Barkley, I attempted to identify a few of the actual off trail obstacles that Laz puts into the races. Of course there were no real maps available of past Barkley races, because there are no real maps distributed to the runner. The course is made up by Laz and is revealed to the runners on a single large map. The runners then have a limited amount of time to copy the details onto their personal maps of the park. There is a cut scene in the documentary that shows some of the course layout. I thought I was going to have to pause the movie and take a stab at sketching it out; however I lucked out though a Google image search. In 2014, the Barkley Fall Classic was started as a race for people that couldn't make the invitation cut for the full Barkley, but wanted the experience of running a full "loop" plus some. It is a marathon and 50K that is run in September. From what I can tell it works like a normal race, real entry fees that go to charity (instead of $1.60 and a pack of dress socks), an actual start time (instead of a random conch blow and lit cigarette), and hundreds of runners (instead of a few dozen). Since the Classic functions like a normal race, there are real maps distributed. The Google search found an image of the 2015 course, with the locations of landmarks such as "Testicle Spectacle", "Rat Jaw", "Big Rat", and "The Hole", all vaguely marked.

So I hatched this idea for a trip. We would set out to cover at least 25 miles of trail, roughly half the miles in the park, over two days. As a bonus, we would attempt at least one of the real Barkley routes if we could safely identify it. Day one, around 15 miles, would be a southern loop, along the length of the Chimney Tops Trail, to the Lookout Tower, then down to the Old Prison Mine Trail, while maybe trying to find the "Rat Jaw". Then we would re-trace back to South Old Mac Trail and follow it back to the campground near the visitor center where we would have a dump out camp. We would grill out steaks and have a grand time. The next day, around 10 miles, would be a northern loop, going west about 3 miles or so up the Lookout Tower West Trail, do a side trip to Bald Knob, and then follow the Cumberland Trail east to Castle Rock and follow the Bird Mountain trail south back to the campground. I was excited about this part because I would be able to experience another portion of the Cumberland Trail. According to the most recent maps I have, this portion is still not connected with the remainder of the sections. It was going to be a whirlwind tour, and I knew there would not be much daylight. I thought if we had some halfway decent weather, we could pull it off.

Of course, I kept saying "we" in the above paragraph, like there was going to be a whole running club of nut jobs lining up to join this excursion. In reality, only my friend from Knoxville, Rob, was crazy enough to accompany me. We began some initial planning on going in November and December, but ultimately it got pushed into early January. In a way I even told myself that making it a winter trip would give it some more credibility, being that we could possibly see Frozen Head Mountain in the state of its namesake, with snow and ice along its iconic rocky face.

Now, what I described in the paragraph above was the plan that I laid out, and it was a good plan. But the hitch in all of this was that this trip was now a winter trip. Tennessee is one of those Mid-South states, where although it is possible to have bad winter weather in December and March, the vast majority of it occurs in the two months of "real winter", January and February. Even this time period can be wildly unpredictable, with days of single digit lows and heavy snow followed by days of 60 degrees and rain. When timed correctly, winter trips can be some of the best experiences you will ever have in the wilderness. Crowds are non-existent, and you can often go for days without seeing anyone. On overlooks where you would typically find yourself surrounded by selfie snapping tourists, you can find actual solitude. If there is any snow or ice around you can get some really cool pictures in the process. In campsites where you would typically have to fight for reservations months in advance, you can get a permit the day you start and have it all to yourself. The critter factor is much diminished, with the mosquitoes, ticks, and snakes no longer an area for much concern. Even the bigger animal threats are much less, although you should still be careful and hang your food. And if bad weather does occur, the challenge of simply pulling it off is hard to replicate the rest of the year. Hundreds of people tramp all over a peak on a summer day partly because it is easy to do. When it is 5 degrees with snow and ice everywhere, it is a much different equation and a much more satisfying accomplishment.

Of course the challenges are numerous as well. Even getting to the trailhead is a big challenge in itself. Parks in the South are notoriously quick to close gates and roads for almost any amount of snow. You will constantly fight to have liquid water, and typically have to sleep with your water bottle in your sleeping bag in order to have something to drink for breakfast. Most mornings are accompanied with a slight dehydration headache. Daylight is so precious. Day is only from about 7:00 a.m. to 5:00 p.m., and night is 14 hours long. Even if you have a group of early risers, it is difficult to get on the trail before 8:00 a.m. If you want to avoid setting up camp and getting water in the dark, you need to get where you are going realistically by 4:00 p.m. That pretty much leaves 8 hours of actual hiking, which also has to encompass breaks and side trips to points of interest. Compounding the time issue is the condition of the trail, which is often muddy or covered in ice or snow. Sometimes every step forward ends with half a step sliding backwards. In the middle of summer, it is completely possible to backpack over 15 miles in good daylight with relative ease. In the winter, anything over a 10 mile day runs the risk of finishing in the dark, and even that is sometimes hard to achieve.

So it is definitely a high risk and a high reward gamble, one that I have taken many times before. Sometimes we wind up with the most iconic group pictures and the best stories of our lives, and sometimes we wind up shopping with the family at an outlet mall. There is a reason it is called an adventure. You never know what is going to happen.

The weekend for me began on Friday morning with a 6:00 a.m. phone call from the school system telling me that my son's school was cancelled. This kind of surprised me considering that I had been obsessed with checking the forecast all week and had been watching the chance of snow decrease significantly for both home and Wartburg. I looked outside and there was a good inch accumulated. It was snowing heavily. The weather folks whiffed on this one. It was 18 degrees, and the temperature was going to remain below freezing until sometime Monday afternoon. Whatever fell was going to hang around for a while.

I had already planned for the cold (and dry) weather, so the arrival of the snow did not greatly affect my plans, but I did decide to wear my heavy backpacking boots while packing my trail runners. Part of this was plain concern about being prepared if I got stranded on the interstate someway. The snow stopped around mid-morning, and I didn't get on the road until late afternoon. By that time the interstate was completely clear. I talked with Rob on the way, and he said that Knoxville had just gotten a dusting that had pretty much melted. The further east I went the less snow I saw. I wasn't worried at all.

I arrived at Rob's house late in the evening. We made plans to get up around six and leave before the projected 7:00 a.m. sunrise. I saw the snow flurries start around midnight, but I really hoped that they would clear out quickly. They did not. Morning began with a very bleak picture. There was well over 2 inches accumulated already, and it was still snowing hard. It turned out that there was a second system in Alabama that moved north in the night, into the Tennessee Valley, dumping snow everywhere and continuing on into the Appalachians.

Being the eternal optimist I am about hiking trips, I could surmise from the radar that everything was really moving out and to the east, which meant in theory, the further west we went, the less snow there would be. We loaded up my truck up in the dark, driving snow and set out. I was slightly irritated but excited at the same time. This reminded me of the old college days of hiking trips during winter break.

It was a little hairy getting to the interstate, but once we got going west it really wasn't too bad. The right lane was well salted and cleared and the snow seemed to be letting up the further west we traveled. After only about 20 miles of interstate travel we reached the Harriman exit. It was past 7:00 a.m. at this point and still seemed to me to be as dark as midnight. We pulled into a Hardee's to have a leisurely breakfast and let a little more daylight appear. I can handle driving in bad conditions, but it makes it so much better when I can actually see what is in front of me. The restaurant was empty except for police and snow plow drivers. By the time we got done eating and drinking coffee, the snow had totally stopped and the morning was beginning to brighten up to show a clearing sky. There was a sunny day in the works.

Highway 27 had some snow, but it was pretty well tracked up and the driving was easy. When we finally turned off onto Flat Fork Road, there was a bit more snow, but we were so close at this point that the slow driving didn't bother me. The park entrance is right at the foot of the mountains, and the ridges stack and pile above the relatively flat terrain surrounding the ranger stations and camping pavilions. The elevation differences range up to around 2,000 feet, from the floor of the Tennessee Valley at the entrance around 1,300 feet, up to the highest ridges around 3,300 feet. As we wound along the narrow road, the white and gray speckled hills and mountains in front of us were shining brightly in the early morning sun, and I couldn't wait to see what was up there.

As we drove along Flat Fork Road, I was looking for the primitive group camp area. From my understanding, it was the only camping available. The developed campground is closed for the winter on November 1st. We drove past a ranger station and over a narrow bridge to another parking lot which held a couple of vehicles. The road past the parking lot was gated. I expected this. I have had several winter trips before turn into gate dodging exercises that sometimes ended up in total defeat. I don't blame the park service, because in the end, they would be the ones responsible for pulling people out. I still wanted to investigate what the situation was so we turned around and headed back to the ranger station. The ranger inside was very helpful, telling us that he would unlock the gate this afternoon for us and let us go back there and camp (for $23). The only catch would be that he would have to lock the gate behind us, so we would be stuck until morning. Our other option was to haul our stuff into a back country campsite about half a mile from the trailhead. Ultimately, we decided to get on the trail and make the call that afternoon. On the way back to my truck we ran into a younger ranger who was heading out to take pictures. He said that he would be around until 6:30 that evening if we ended up wanting to stay. They did both mention to us that it would be around 5 degrees that night, and it was currently around 0 degrees on the high ridges. That 0 degree number definitely stuck in my head as we were gearing up for the day.

That morning we had made the call to go ahead and put our boots on when we saw the amount of snow that was falling, accepting that there would be no trail running. We both had our day packs absolutely stuffed to capacity. Besides our base layers of running pants, running shirts, and running pullovers that we were wearing, we each had a fleece jacket, a down jacket, and a Gore-Tex jacket. Of course we had hats and gloves, and Rob took his balaclava. I left mine in my in my big pack, which I regretted. We each carried a two liter camel-bak and bags of trail mix. Add to that our head lamps and camera/phones, and there was not a spare piece of unused real estate in either of our day packs. It was in the high teens so we started out wearing our down jackets, knowing that we would shed them in a few minutes of hard uphill going. Rob had brought his trekking poles and we split them. We didn't have to drive anywhere else, the Chimney Tops trailhead was directly behind the ranger station so we headed out, charging up the snowy trail, completely unmarked by foot, paw, or hoof. It was apparent that this morning we were going to have this part of the park to ourselves. This was our reward for braving the horrible roads all morning.

After two or three switchbacks, we shed our down jackets and went with just our running layers. The trail was plenty steep, and we were moving fast enough that we were staying plenty warm. After a while I had to even take off my hat and gloves, but I would put them back on quickly if we stopped for any length of time. The snow was really only a couple of inches deep on the trail, but the trekking pole made a world of difference.

The switchbacks ended as we topped out on a ridge, and the trail began to steeply descend, still heading south. We could clearly see the next ridge we would have to climb, and it seemed significantly bigger than what we had just crossed. At the bottom of the ridge we had a quick rock hop across Rocky Fork Branch. I am always pleased to see an unbridged stream crossing. It seems that more and more bridges are finding their way into the backcountry. A little dancing across mossy rocks never hurt anyone, until you fall face first into a stream in winter, which I have done of course.

We started up the switchbacks for the new ridge. It was also plenty steep and we were having no problem staying warm. I have always had a complicated relationship with the winter woods. They are open and inviting. No impenetrable thickets, no poison ivy patches, just go wherever you want. But the relentless grayness and silence can be oppressive. I have found myself quitting early while deer hunting in late December just because the scenery was bringing me down. But as we were ascending that second ridge around 11:00 a.m. that morning, I was definitely in the rose colored glasses phase. The clouds had been swept away by a stiff north wind, and the sun was shining brighter than I had seen it in weeks. The snow in the woods was so fresh and untouched. We were now following a single set of deer tracks, and the silence of everything was uplifting. I began to wax poetically to Rob about how there was no better place to be on earth. Then we topped out on the ridge, and I got really quiet.

I had noticed how much colder it was getting as we were nearing the top. I had to put my gloves and hat back on. My trick of blowing the water back into my hydration pack after I finished drinking to prevent the hose from freezing was starting to not work so well. The hose kept freezing up, and I had to work on it for a minute or so to get water flowing again. When we did top the ridge and the full force of the wind hit us, I swear it dropped another 10 degrees in about 3 seconds. The view of the rolling ridges continuing northeast and the snow covered rolling hills and scattered fields of the Tennessee Valley directly below us, was beautiful. But conditions being what they were, we couldn't devote much attention to it. I took off my gloves to dig into my pack to get a bag of food and retrieve my fleece jacket. After three handfuls of food, I had to put my gloves back on because my hands were getting numb. My cheeks began to burn as well. Neither one of us were saying a word, which is typically a really bad sign.

After choking down as much food as we could as quick as we could, we turned back to the trail, which was now following the crest of the ridge eastward. My hands were still numb inside my gloves. I felt warmer with the fleece jacket, but I made the decision that if after ten minutes of hard going, my hands were not better, we would have to turn around and go back. Fortunately, there was plenty of hard going to be had. The trail began to climb a very steep rise in the ridge top. The snow had accumulated much deeper here, with some drifts of about 18 inches. The trail was hard to find and every step held the potential of sliding backwards further than the actual step taken. We were using the trekking poles more like ice axes now. Without them we would have had no shot at proceeding any further. As we got nearer to what looked like the top, I definitely got some summit fever and pushed even harder. My hands were starting to feel good again, and I didn't want to risk them getting numb. I also was pleased in my choice of boots because my feet were staying warm. I was halfway beginning to think that we could actually pull this off safely.

I reached the rocky ramparts of the ridge top and finally took a break. My water hose was completely frozen now. Rob had put on his balaclava and I was really kicking myself for not bringing mine, but my cheeks had gotten better with the hard work of the ridge. The ramparts were very steep and the trail stayed to the left of them. In good weather I would have tried to climb on top, but in the conditions, it just wasn't worth it.

We followed the side of the rocky bluffs, stopping for a moment under a large overhang which offered nice shelter from the wind. At the saddle after the ramparts, we climbed onto a boulder to take some pictures. My camera had been fully charged, but in the cold it would not turn to picture mode. We tried our phones. They had been fully charged too. They turned on for five or ten seconds before dying. Apparently we were outside the zone of temperature where electronics reliably work. I hoped we would not find the same situation with our headlamp batteries if we ended up needing them.

The trail stayed on the crest of the ridge, with an occasional drop or rise and rocky scramble along a boulder strewn stretch. The going would have been pretty fast, but the snow drifts were more frequent. I was really getting annoyed at the idea of us not having any pictures. I thought for a minute about trying to warm up the camera next to my skin and started to lift up the layers of my clothes. I kept pulling at my undershirt and didn't understand why it was tucked in. Then I realized that it wasn't my shirt I was touching, it was my skin that was numbed from the cold. Oh well, feeling in your abdomen isn't that important anyway. Then I actually got smart and took the battery pack out of the camera and rubbed in my hands and blew on it for a good minute. It worked and we started to get some decent pictures. The camera stayed in my jacket pocket the rest of the trip, and it kept working. Our phones never warmed enough to work.

We could see the mountains through the trees because it was winter, but there were not many decent overlooks. It was getting on past 1:00 p.m. when we reached Mart Fields campsite. We first came to an old chimney used as a fire pit at a wide spot in the trail, and then we came to larger cluster of campsites spread along the wide crest of the ridge. We were both getting a little concerned about time. From the slow driving to the park and the conversations with the rangers, to the struggling through the drifts and checking to make sure we weren't losing our hands; the cold and the snow had really messed up our time table. We had only gone 5 miles in 3 hours. I had made a modified goal for us of the Lookout Tower on Frozen Head Mountain, but we were starting to have our doubts about making it. We decided to push on towards the Spicewood Trail junction and make the call then.

The trail turned north and lost some altitude, but still managed to stay on top of the ridge somewhat, or at least just under the crest. We were really booking it now, but I was getting worried that it was too little too late. We covered the mile quick, clearly seeing the trail descend into a saddle and then climb the steep rise to the far mountain top where we assumed the summit of Frozen Head and the Lookout Tower stood.

At the bottom of the saddle was the junction with the Spicewood Trail. The Chimney Top Trail clearly continued steeply to the northeast. The Spicewood Trail went west and down, back towards the park entrance, just under 3 miles away. If we had continued on towards the Lookout Tower, it would have been over a mile to the tower trail spur (steep uphill), then 0.8 to the tower and back (at least half uphill), then nearly 3.5 miles back along the South Old Mac Trail. It was after 2:00 p.m. at this point, meaning that there were only 2 good hours of daylight left, especially once we got deeper into the narrow valley. We ultimately decided that the smart thing to do would be to head back the quicker way along Spicewood and save the Lookout Tower for another day. As much as I hated to do it, risking the travel in the dark when it was going to be close to 0 degrees was just not worth it. We took a decent break for cold weather, a good five minutes, even taking the time to attach my mini tripod onto the trail sign for a "group" picture.

I have to admit that I was decently bummed out over missing the Lookout Tower. It was kind of the final little failure in the whole trail running trip idea that had totally flopped. Thankfully, my dreary attitude was soon lifted by the magnificence of our new surroundings. The trail continued westward, cut into a very steep mountainside, and overlooks into the narrow valley to the north of us were scattered along the right side of the trail. The snow was deeper here and totally untouched, not even deer tracks. We actually struggled to distinguish between the trail and the snow covered creek beds several times. Of course this reinforced the reasoning behind trying to get out in the daylight. Making those kind of distinctions with a headlamp would have been miserable. The trail turned north and started losing elevation quickly. By 3:30 p.m., the sun was below the ridge to our south and the woods seemed to be entering into dusk. We soon reached the intersection of the South Old Mac Trail as well as Judge Branch Creek. Turning left on to South Old Mac, the path was now a wide Jeep trail, and we joined several sets of tracks leading back towards the trailhead and parking lot.

After a few minutes of strolling down this wide lane we came into the trailhead parking area where there were still a couple of cars parked. We walked down the road back to the ranger station while talking over our options. The whole prospect of staying out in weather near 0 degrees was seeming less and less fun. The campsite was going to be still covered in snow, making fire building difficult. The whole idea of covering 25 miles of trail in two days was completely shot now. Even if we stayed another day, the best we could manage would be another loop like we just did, and maybe not even that long. Then on top of it all, our vehicles would be locked behind a gate until dawn. Ultimately, we decided to head back to

Knoxville. We got cleaned up at Rob's house and went on a self-guided tour of Knoxville's emerging micro-brewery scene. As much as I hate to have a trip not turn out as I plan, I will say that the evening on the town was much more comfortable than squatting in the snow while trying to grill a half frozen steak over a pit. I guess I am getting soft.

Even though it wound up being a late night, we did get a good trail run in Sunday morning. We ran a couple of good routes in the snow covered trails around the rock quarry in the Ijams Nature Center. In better conditions, and without the lingering effects of a brewery tour, you could run for days on the interconnecting trails that span across this area that is only three miles from downtown Knoxville. I bet we could do 50 miles. And so another crazy trip idea is born.

Chimney Top Trail to Spicewood is the most southern loop on this map.

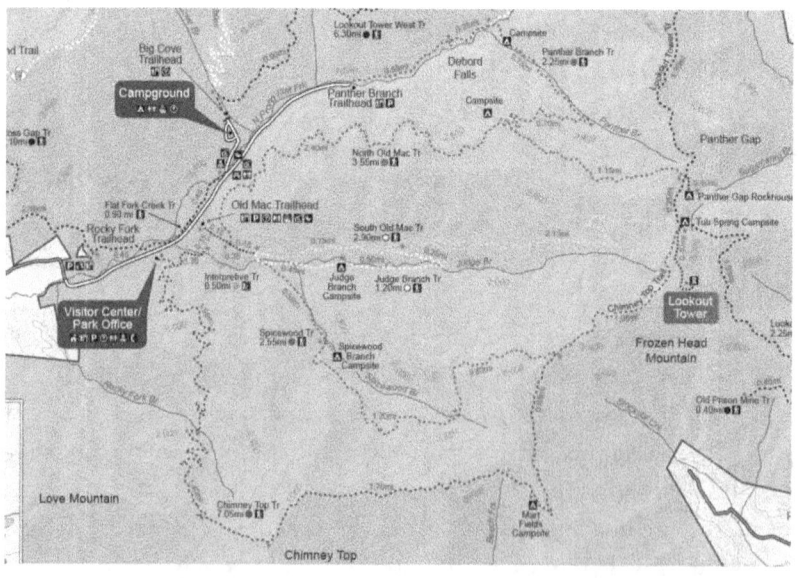

Chapter III

Cumberland Trail – Obed River Gorge

Before I start this chapter and introduce the Obed River, I need to introduce the Cumberland Trail. The Cumberland Trail is a work in progress. When completed in Tennessee, it will cover an approximate 300 mile span along the eastern escarpment of the Cumberland Plateau, with Cumberland Gap National Historic Park on the northern end and Chickamagua and Chattanooga National Military Park on the southern end. In Tennessee, the trail corridor is overseen by the Justin P. Wilson Cumberland Trail State Park, but it is contained on public land under different types of management, including other State Parks, Wildlife Management Areas, National Park Service managed areas, and Wild and Scenic River areas. Regulations about camping vary greatly, and there are not decent overnight routes on many sections yet. As of this writing, the trail is about two thirds completed. It is a piece of the Great Eastern Trail, which when completed will span nine states, connecting trail systems on the Florida/Alabama border to trail systems in New York state, while staying slightly west of the Appalachian Trail. The idea is to create another great thru-hike challenge to hopefully take pressure off the Appalachian Trail. This endeavor is being primarily managed by nonprofit conversation groups throughout the states where the trail is being is built. In Tennessee, the Cumberland Trails Conference is heading up the majority of the trail construction as well as the promotion of the existing routes. Their website; www.cumberlandtrail.org, is where you can see maps and descriptions of the 14 segments, updates on construction and trail conditions, donate to the cause, or volunteer to join a construction crew. The Obed River Section is one of the three sections in which I have experience, and I have plenty of plans to work down the list. By the way, if you have any future aspirations about being the first one to thru-hike the Great Eastern Trail, you are too late. Joanna Swanson and Bart Houck made the first official thru-hike in 2013, making use of existing trails that follow the intended route, and I guess making their own way when there was no trail at all. Sorry, I was disappointed at the missed opportunity as well.

After I started to pay attention to the Cumberland Plateau and began planning trips, I always had thoughts of doing something with the Obed River involved. The Obed flows from just south of Crossville on a 45 mile long eastern arch that ends by joining the Emory River, which flows into the Clinch River, which flows in Watts Bar Lake. It crosses under Interstate 40, but it is virtually impossible to see the water because the gorge is so deep. It is one the wildest rivers left in South and Tennessee's only Federally designated Wild and Scenic River (and one of only three in the Southeast). Unlike almost every other river in Tennessee, it is not controlled by dams, although it was almost dammed up in the 1960's. The project was ended after a protracted political battle. Because it is remote and wild, if you want a whitewater experience on it, you have to figure it out yourself. While the Obed River and Daddy's Creek drainages contain premium Class IV and V rapids, there are no commercial guide services that operate on it. So for a long time I had aspirations of somehow running a less serious section in a canoe, kayak, or raft. You can find some pretty decent descriptions on the internet of trips that others have taken, but I decided that before I even tried to organize such an endeavor, I needed to see the river first hand. Other than stopping my car in the middle of I-40 and looking over the edge of the bridge, a hiking trip was my only option, and there just happened to be a section of the Cumberland Trail that ran along the gorge.

In the Spring of 2013, I started to do some research. The only maps I could obtain were on the Cumberland Trail website. Currently there are two segments of the CT open in this area, the Obed Gorge Section and the Emory River Section. They are connected by a road. The Emory River Section is just 1.3 miles long and abruptly ends after an overlook. The Obed Section stretches between Daddy's Creek and the Nemo Bridge. It is 14.1 miles long and there is parking at each trailhead. The 2.4 miles between Alley Ford and Nemo is on Federal lands managed by the National Park Service. The rest of the trail is located in the Catoosa Wildlife Management Area, controlled by the State. There is camping at Alley Ford and the Nemo trailhead. There is no legal backcountry camping in the Wildlife Management Area. In this story, we broke the rules. In our defense, at the time the websites that I was using to plan the trip did not say backcountry camping was not allowed, and I even saw a map that had a couple of camping sites marked along the river. It was not until we actually started hiking that we saw a sign on the trail saying that there was no camping. The plans were already made, so we risked it.

I have a lot of conflicting feelings about this. On one hand, I understand that in the Eastern U.S., we have a lot of people. And if we are going to continue to have places worth going to, people have to go to them so they support their continued protection. And if we are going to have a lot of people going into these places, we have to make rules to keep them from completely wrecking the place. I have always tried to be extremely respectful of where I camp, and there have only been a very few instances where I camped in a place where I wasn't really supposed to. I have never built a fire ring or even not built a fire at all if there wasn't evidence of one being there before. I have buried my fire ashes, scattered limbs and sticks back over the site, roughed leaves back up that we tromped down, and even propped plants and grasses back up before we left. I also realize that even if you could get away with it, there are just places that are so special that you should not camp there. Even though I have stumbled upon others doing it, I would never plop down a tent in the middle of Spence Field, Gregory Bald, or the LeConte cliff tops in the Smokies. If you are going to camp illegally, at least have the decency to go a few hundred yards away in the woods. These places have needs that will always trump your desire for a sense of exploring freedom. If you really want camping freedom, go out west, where you can still pretty much plop down anywhere.

However; I will have to admit, that the lack of backcountry camping on the CT bothers me. I don't understand the point of building a trail that is supposed to be another great thru-hiking mecca, when you don't allow a few designated back country sites, at least along the most popular sections. If people want a little seclusion and they're willing to put in some work, put up with the cold or heat or bugs, struggle with water sources, and eat food cooked in an aluminum pouch, you should give them a place to go. Especially when there are already sites there. I believe the campsites that were marked on the map I saw, and the one we ended up finding to stay in, were made by kayakers doing overnight trips on the river. It was the river runners that put a lot of the work into keeping the whole place from turning into a lake, and in my opinion, they should be able to take a few days to enjoy it. Also, I have a hard time understanding how the hiking restrictions during hunting season in the Wildlife Management Areas will work with the eventual through hikers. The section of trail that we were on in the Catoosa WMA is closed weekends from Mid-October through December, then the whole months of February and March, then most of April to the first week of May. I have hunted all of my life and I don't see how hikers and hunters can't share the same spot. In the hours that are good for hunting, there really shouldn't be hikers out. If the hunters just treat the trail like they would a public road, then it really shouldn't be a safety problem either. I am sure these issues will get sorted out eventually.

So, ultimately I present this story with a warning, if you try to find one of these sites, know that you run the risk of getting caught by a ranger and being made to move. A good step you can take to avoid this situation is not actually unpack your tent until almost sunset, which greatly lowers the chance of someone stumbling onto you. Also, pick up after yourself impeccably, and make the place look better than it looked before you. Pretend like you are Anthony Hopkins in *Remains of the Day*, just in the woods. So iron the leaves, arrange the sticks in a random pattern, and prop the honeysuckle vines back up. What about the poison ivy? Best to leave it be.

This was going to end up being a summer trip, the first one I had been on in a while. Summer trips have some special parts that you just can't get in other times of the year. The extra hours of daylight allow you cover more ground. If you don't want to cover more ground, you have time to lounge around camp in the daylight or at minimum cover all your camp chores, such as wood gathering and cooking, when you can actually see what you are doing. There is also time for extra credit hikes, which are additional excursions you do with a light pack after you reach your initial camp.

When I started to look at options for this hike I quickly realized that it was going to be an "out and back" hike. On most sections of the CT, you are going to end up with an "out and back" hike. There are few options for loops. The only other option is to set a vehicle at one trailhead, drive to another trailhead, hike to your second vehicle, then retrieve your first vehicle. When I first started planning trips, I loved setting up these convoluted schemes. The most extreme ever involved a trip in the Smokies were we hiked from a car parked at Fontana Dam to a car parked in Cades Cove. It was probably around 25 miles between the vehicles as a crow flies but took us nearly two hours by road, and then two hours more to get the other vehicle, and then around two hours more to get back to a major highway. Needless to say, in my older age and with less disposable time, I would rather be in the woods than spend additional hours in the car and try to hike loops or "out and backs" as much as I can.

The plan for this hike was to start on the southwestern end of the Obed Gorge Section and hike towards the Nemo trailhead to the northeast. The reason I choose the Daddys Creek Trailhead versus the northeastern one was simply because it appeared to be accessed quicker from I-40. Because there were no clear camps marked on the map, we were simply going to hike around 4 hours or so, find a campsite, then gear up with daypacks and continue on the trail until we felt like turning around or realized there was nothing else to see within a realistic walking distance. I have found these type of hikes are great for places where you don't know the terrain very well and want to explore the area as much as possible. If you get turned around or just lose a lot of altitude with the trail, it is a lot easier to find yourself or recover altitude when you are not carrying 35 to 40 pounds on your back. It is also a good way to scout for future hikes.

The final roster for this trip was Jack, my friend from Jackson, and Rob. Jack and I set out from Jackson, headed West on I-40, around 5:45 a.m. and rendezvoused with Rob at the Crossville exit 322. For some reason or other we did not car pool and caravanned north on Peavine Road (for 1.8 miles), trying to locate Firetower Road on our left. We only had to turn around once before we found it and were on our way to the trailhead. By the way, if you are ever doing searches for directions to a place involving a Firetower Road, take care to make sure it is near the intended destination. There are no less than 10,000 Firetower Roads in the U.S. and Canada. Your GPS could take you to Nova Scotia.

The asphalt ended after two miles, and then it was dusty gravel. Plumes of white dust rising 15 feet in the air enveloped us. We passed the gate to the Catoosa Wildlife Management Area and continued on through the rolling terrain typical on the Plateau. Most of the forest had been select cut recently, with wide areas of brush between the lonely, surviving trees. In some areas the woods would be all new growth, unpenetrated by light. In some areas there were the scars of forest fires. In some places there were small cultivated fields with neat rows that had been freshly planted. Portions of this land are in the process of being converted back to oak savanna with native grasses (pre-European settler days), and there are signs marking the progress. There were deep tractor tracks in the dusty gravel along the entire length of the road. There were also what looked like ATV trails shooting off the main road in all directions and winding into the distant hills. It was apparent that this land was heavily managed by the TWRA (Tennessee Wildlife Resources Agency) with the goal of providing public hunting grounds. It was definitely not a National Park, but anything is better than a golf course, shopping mall, or housing development. Despite all the evidence of human activity, we saw no people, vehicles, or structures, and the woods continued to get more dense and we drove deeper into the reserve. Near the end of the 15 miles, the road dipped into a deep gulley of Daddys Creek and followed along a single lane wooden bridge. There was a parking area off to the right, which was empty. Beside the parking area the creek became wide, and there was a rocky shore. A small spring came off a nearby bluff, forming a small waterfall. It looked like a great place to swim, fish, or just sit and watch. We did not have time for any of those. As we were trying to find the trailhead, our solitude was cracked a little by an approaching dust plume and crunching gravel. A truck pulled up in the parking area, and a dad and son got out and began to get dressed to swim. I was relieved that we were at least going to have the first part of the hike to ourselves instead of playing leap frog with another group.

We found the trailhead sign a little before 11:00 a.m. The morning was definitely wearing thin. As I mentioned earlier, there was a sign saying that the only backcountry camping was at Alley Ford, at least 11 miles away. That wasn't happening so we pressed on. We had all opted to wear long pants, and I was soon glad for it. The trail was very rough and overgrown, which is typically a good sign that you aren't going to encounter crowds. The trail crossed a road after 0.2 miles and then dropped steeply into Daddy's Creek Gorge. It was initially so steep that we took a while to discern what was trail and what was a washed out section of slope. This was the first of dozens of trail finding endeavors in which we would engage in over the next two days. It was very steep, and the boulders that made the trail were unstable. We descended for a while, then we would climb again. We could hear Daddys Creek below us, but somewhere during our descent it faded away. About halfway down one of the longer stair stepped pitches, Rob spotted a coiled up copperhead in the middle of the one of the steps. He pointed it out as he side stepped the whole rock. Jack saw it immediately too. It took me a good ten more seconds of scanning the trial until I spotted it, which really irritated me. I am usually a pretty good snake spotter, even with copperheads, who are notoriously well camouflaged and completely aware of it, staying totally still when most other snakes would scatter with an approaching vibration. I typically don't worry too much about snakes as long as I am on a well-worn path, going with the idea that creatures that spend their whole lives lying flat on the ground are pretty good about not getting trampled on, but often copperheads are kind of an exception. While running I have high hurdled over many of those little buggers stretched out on the road. One time hiking down from Old Rag in Shenadohah National Park with my friend Brian, I spotted a copperhead stretched out in the trail about three feet in front of me and jumped clear to the side, yelling "copperhead" as I flew through the air. Brian had no idea what I was saying and continued on until I yelled at him to freeze and take a couple steps back. The snake was six inches in front of him, and he still couldn't see it until we walked around at a different angle. So this one in the boulder field definitely made me take my steps a little more careful, especially if I was leading.

When the trail leveled out there were two spur trails leading to a cliff top overlook of the gorge below us. They gave us good views of the whitewater below and the bluffs on the opposing side of the gorge. Far to the north we could the see the drop in the ridge that had to be the junction at the Obed River. Daddys Creek was about 500 feet below us. The gorge was typical of most Plateau gorges, sharp sandstone bluffs at the top, then a steep, wooded slope down to the boulder lined creek bed. The trees were mostly hardwood, which meant that there had been surprisingly little clear cutting in the area. In the East, a typical protected forest area is a place where every indigenous hardwood tree was clear cut, and the land was reclaimed by planting fast growing pines. The car sized boulders in the stream were bordered with small rapids. I was eager to get down to them for a closer view. After pictures, we the hit trail again, making good time despite the rough route. For the next couple of miles the trail stayed at the foot of a bluff which had numerous overhangs, including a cave like structure called Rain House. At this point in the trip, I was amazed at the lack of trash or graffiti we had seen. Not only had we not seen a person, we had not seen a sign that anyone had ever been around, not even a roughed up boot track in the leaves. The trail rolled along the foot of the bluff until it descended down into the gorge again. I thought we would see the confluence of Daddys Creek and the Obed, but we never caught a glimpse of the water. After a relatively flat span, we finally got a chance to access the river along a rocky bank. We scrambled out onto a large flat boulder in the middle of the stream and took our packs off for a good break. Upstream, just in the bend of the river, was the end of a pretty rough looking stretch of rapids. The water around us was calm and clear and we even spotted a few fish hanging out in the eddy of a rocky outcrop on the opposing bank. The heavily timbered sides of the gorge were the bright shades of green that only happen in May and June, before the hot spells of July and August burn and dim them. The sun was warm and there was a cool breeze off the rushing water. I could have stayed there all day.

After a few pictures we put on our packs and got back to it. The trail climbed again, and we found ourselves traveling along a pass between a bluff below and a bluff above. There were steel rods hammered into the rock for some purpose. I think we were traveling on an old railroad bed, the track long moved away. We found a wide spot in the trail with a couple nice large logs for our lunch break. I prefer to stop for meals at well marked landmarks, such as overlooks or stream crossings. These good stopping places provide both a little reward for our work and an easy to understand waypoint on the trip plan. In this case there was no such spot, and we were hungry. After lunch, the trail turned south and crossed Turkey Creek (beside a small waterfall) along a very nicely built bridge and then turned back north, crossing another small bridge. Up until now it had not been very hot, but soon it turned muggy as we moved away from the main gorge. As soon as the trail brought us out of the Turkey Creek drainage things cooled off quick. It was getting on past 2:00 p.m., and we really needed to find a campsite soon. We walked slowly now, just scanning the surrounding landscape for some sign of a flat place big enough to fit two tents. Another 30 minutes passed and I was getting worried. The place I had seen on the internet map marked "camp" had been impossible to pin point. In the heavy undergrowth of summer, it would have been very easy to have strolled by without noticing it. We could see the river below us occasionally, but from the trail it was just a steep, rocky slope for a good 200 feet that abruptly ended in the roaring water.

Rob was leading now and suddenly stopped and pointed down the embankment which seemed a little more wooded and less steep. At the edge of the river there were a couple of sandy flat spots and a fire ring.

There were even some rocks along the bank that extended out in the river, making a good spot for filtering water. It was not a great looking place due to the lack of easy access to get there from the trail, but we had to take it. There was no telling if we would see another spot near us, and if we were going to have any chance to explore deeper with our afternoon day hike we had to find a camp very soon. Leaving the trail, we half slid, half fell, half stumbled down the leaf covered boulders, mud, and scree, grabbing handfuls of tree limbs and trying to avoid briar patches as much as possible. And yes, I was thinking the whole time about that copperhead. When we finally got to the bottom, it looked workable. There was a flat area about 15 yards wide that extended a 100 yards or so along the river, between the water the steep hill slope. Most of it was overgrown with briars, rhododendron, and cane, but there was just enough cleared space for our camp to fit. I was definitely not looking forward to climbing up that slope with a full pack on, but that would be tomorrow morning anyway. Right now we had work to do. I had lashed a small machete on my pack just in case we needed a cutting tool. I very carefully cleared a little of the worst part of the poison ivy, which was mainly centered around a decaying tree stump in the middle of the sandy beach. It was a little bit of a risk with the camping restrictions to set our tents up, but we had neither seen nor heard anyone all day. After we gathered fire wood, easily found along the bank, and hung our packs. We packed our daypacks for our afternoon of much easier walking. I got to use my REI Flash pack for the first time. I really like bringing auxiliary bags that pack flat and weigh very little. Even if you don't end up on an extra-curricular day hike, they still can be used a myriad of ways, even hanging food.

After struggling and sliding up the slope again to the trail, we followed the river for about another mile through some long confusing switchbacks to Anvil Rock, which as the name suggests, was a big boulder shaped like an anvil, forming an overhang off the top of the gorge bluff. There were steel pegs in a tree next to it, and Rob and I climbed on top. It was really not much of a view. The trees completely blocked any glimpse of the water below us. I realized that it was getting on near 5:00 p.m. and we needed to head back. (After reading the current online CT guide, I now realize that there was a pretty good overlook not far down the trail, but again, at the time I had very limited information.) It had been an overall disappointing day hike, but you never know until you go. It was better than sitting in camp anyway. The day was wearing on near 6:00 p.m. when we were nearing our camp area. The wind had apparently blown away a piece of tape we had tried to use as a marker for the spot on the trail where we needed to descend. The sun had moved lower to the edge of the gorge rim, and now the shadows below were darker along the bank of the river. Nothing looked the same as it had two hours ago. After walking for a while we started to get an uneasy feeling and knew we had passed it. We turned around and backtracked for 10 minutes. I was starting to get worried. Yes we had left the car keys in the camp, that is a no-no. Suddenly Rob stopped ahead and pointed down toward the river. The camp was barely visible in the shadows. If we had not set up our tents, I am not sure if we could have seen it at all. We quickly slid back down to camp before it disappeared again. This situation reminded me of the extreme care that needs to be taken when packing for such an extracurricular hike. Because you never really know what can happen that will get you separated from all of your gear, at minimum take along:

1) A little food
2) At least half a day's worth of water
3) Knife
4) Compass
5) Map
6) Lighter
7) First Aid Kit
8) Rain Jacket/Second Layer
9) Cell Phone (and camera)
10) Headlamp/Batteries
11) The Freaking Car Keys

We scrambled out onto the river boulders to get water. The Flash pack also proved very handy at hauling back everyone's water. We got a fire started relatively easily. While hunting for more firewood I did find a partially buried beer can, which I packed out. It was the only trash I saw over the course of the two days. We cooked dinner just as the sun was going down over the edge of the ridge across the river. Darkness arrived very quickly. My meal was a Chinese shrimp noodle bowl which surprisingly turned out to be incredibly good. We had drug flat rocks around the fire for places to sit. We stayed up very late talking and enjoying the finer spoils of camp. Around midnight we ran out of things to say and retired to the tents, drifting off to the sound of the rushing Obed just twenty feet away. It must have gotten down in the 50's that night, because I went to sleep in my fleece bag and woke up freezing about 2:00 am. I put another shirt on and went back to sleep quickly.

I woke up at dawn. We had not put the rainfly on the tent so when I sat up, the river was directly in my view through the mesh windows of the tent. I believe this was my best wake up view ever. I scrambled out on the boulders in the edge of the water and took some pictures upstream as the rising sun was lighting up the opposing ridge over the river, while the water and the rocks below were still in dawn's shadow. It is hard to believe that if not for the effort of a few people, this whole majestic scene would be buried at the bottom of a lake. How many more places like this in Tennessee now sit under hundreds of feet of water? Will we ever have the will to bring them back?

It took a while for everyone to get moving, but we did pretty good, even taking time to filter more water and make coffee. None of us were looking forward to the climb back to the trail, but by 9:00 a.m. we left our little camp and scrambled back up the slope again. We made very good time on the trail and covered the ground quicker climbing than when we were descending. My copperhead friend had moved on, but I was looking pretty hard for him. We took one real break at the Rain House, one picture break at Blueberry Cove overlook, and one lost detour that only cost us about ten minutes. We hoofed it the rest of the way and got back to the road around noon. When we came out of the woods into the parking lot, it was filled with cars and the creek was filled with families swimming. These were the first people we had seen since the morning before. We drove down the dusty path back to I-40 and ate a quick victory meal at the Crossville exit Hardee's.

During the trip, it had not been very warm, and we were not bothered by mosquitoes. For the most part, I don't have a problem with bugs on summer trips. Usually we are moving too much in the daytime, and the campfire smoke keeps them down at night. On this trip I had carried repellent, but I had not used it because we really did not see that many mosquitoes, not even by the river. After we got back I realized that I had made a terrible mistake. It wasn't the flying insects that got me, it was the ground dwelling chiggers that were all over the leaf covered trail that we shuffled through for two days. If I had just sprayed my shoes and legs, it would have gone a long way in preventing the 75 to 100 chigger bites I found on my legs, as well as the five or so ticks I pulled off me. I also ended up getting two bad patches of poison ivy.

So after several weeks of recovery (and two rounds of steroids for the poison ivy), I decided that I needed to alter my summer hiking strategy. Ultimately, I need to wear boots instead of trail shoes and liberally bathe in DEET. Other than the self-inflicted wounds, it was a fun trip that we were able to enjoy in isolation that is rarely achieved in the Eastern U.S. this day in time. But what about the scouting for the canoe trip? (a.k.a -the motivation for the whole trip) After seeing firsthand the rapids on Daddys Creek and the Obed, and watching a couple of videos online about people that canoed the same section we had just walked beside, the official verdict is that a future self-guided canoe trip would be completely insane. Of course, that doesn't mean we won't try it down the road somewhere.

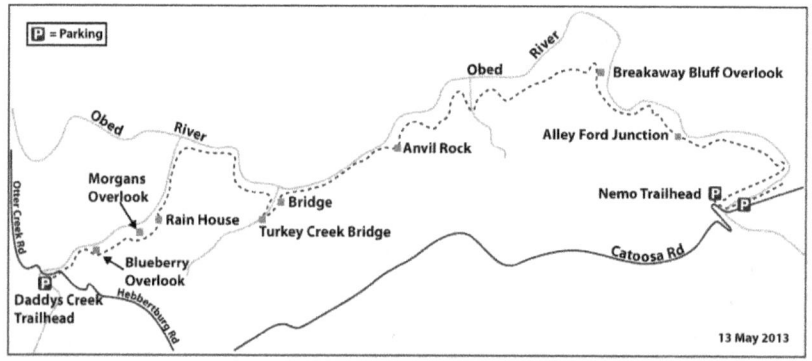

Chapter IV

Cumberland Trail – Grassy Cove

Of all of the trips described in this book, this one is by far the easiest place to access and quickest payoff for the effort. If you are driving I-40 between Knoxville and Nashville, you can take exit 329 south on Battown Road, take a right on Black Mountain Road, park, hike for couple hundred yards, and stand on top of wide, sheer sandstone bluffs overlooking Grassy Cove as well as the entire Tennessee Valley. This whole Black Mountain endeavor is about a 15 minute detour off the interstate. Even if you end your trip there and don't continue hiking the CT, it is well worth it.

Grassy Cove is a small valley just to the east of Crossville that is geologically similar to the Sequatchie Valley, which cuts a much larger swath through the southern half of the Plateau. Grassy Cove is walled in by Brady Mountain to the west, Bear Den Mountain to the east, and Black Mountain to the north. The Cove is drained through streams that all end underground. The water flows through a system of caves to eventually form the head waters of the Sequatchie River. The Cumberland Trail section in this area follows the ridges of Black Mountain and Brady Mountain. This particular story involves a short day hike along the Black Mountain portion, which spans 3.6 miles from the parking lot described above, to the Brady Mountain trailhead/ Cox Valley Road trailhead on Highway 68. The southern part of this section goes south from the Brady Mountain trailhead for 7.8 miles to connect with a trailhead on Jewett Road (see cover photo). Past Jewett Road there is a two mile section under construction that will connect the CT into Sequatchie State Park.

My visit to this section of the CT came about as an extracurricular venture connected with my trip to run in a trail half-marathon at Fall Creek Falls State Park. My dad was going with me to the race, and I was wanting to find a spot for us to get in a decent hike in a place we had not been before. I have a pretty much have standing policy that anytime I am near any type of natural landscape that might contain the slightest possibility of a decent adventure, I find a way to see what is out there. Over the years, I have had a few strike outs, such as closed parks or greenways that are on maps but haven't been built yet, but for the most part I have personally discovered some pretty cool places. If you have some decent shoes, a bottle of water, and a couple of hours, you will be amazed at the trouble you can get into.

In the fall of 2010 I had been training for the Fall Creek Falls Trail Half Marathon since early August. The weather was sickeningly hot basically the entire time. By the middle of October, we had not seen rain in over 45 days and temperatures were about 15 degrees above normal. I normally get pretty burned out before a race, but this weather took it to a whole new level. I was looking forward to the race, but I was also needing to get into the woods for a bit to decompress.

On Saturday morning, my dad and I left Jackson around 9:00 a.m. The weather had finally turned perfect, not a cloud in the sky and high's in the 60's. We reached the Crossville exit a little before 2:00 p.m., and after making a quick stop for gas, we headed south on a very narrow, winding country road. The directions off the internet led us true as we quickly found ourselves ascending Black Mountain Road, which was about as narrow as a driveway. We left the open farm country and now only thick trees bordered the road as it steeply climbed. We had probably entered the Black Mountain State Natural Area, but there were no signs until we reached a parking lot beside a cell tower. It had taken us less than fifteen minutes from the interstate exit. The parking lot was full of cars. We grabbed our day packs and headed towards the trailhead. I was carrying my old camel bak with some food shoved down beside the water bladder. My dad had the EMS travel daypack that I had given him for Christmas some years earlier. The trail entered the woods, and we soon came to an old well house and stone chimney. We started a steep climb that soon leveled off. After a few hundred yards we saw an overlook sign pointing to a spur trail. The spur descended a short rocky slope and entered the craggy ramparts of the eastern escarpment of the Cumberland Plateau. We crossed a small foot bridge and stepped onto large slabs of exposed rock that formed the cliff tops. In a front of us were sweeping views of Grassy Cove and the Tennessee Valley beyond. We could see the blue line of the Tennessee River and the puffing cooling towers of the Watts Bar power plant. Closer to us were the rolling pastures of Grassy Cove, and on the far horizon we could see the soft, blue shadows of the Smokies. Full disclosure here, the atmospheric conditions were incredibly clear, typically the view is probably much more hazy.

The slabs of rock on the cliff tops were broken into large blocks with 20 to 30 foot deep fissures between them. Most of the cracks were 3 feet or less in width, probably jumpable if you wanted to. The surface of the rock was pock marked and indented with fossils, looking like it should lie next to the pounding surf on some Maine beach. The colors were near peak in the forest surrounding us, but were really only getting started in the valley below. We took lots of pictures anyway, and after about twenty minutes or so, headed back to the loop trail. We were not heading back to the parking lot with all of the other camera toting crowd. We were heading west on the loop, towards the start of this CT section.

After a few minutes of walking along the flat ridge, we followed the CT as it split west off the loop. The trail wound through an old grown up field and then to a steep slope and a rock stair case which descended through a narrow crack between two gigantic slabs of rock. These slabs formed cliffs about 30 to 40 feet tall on the downhill side. When we reached the bottom, there were more slabs towering in front of me, forming a kind of maze. We ran into several rock climbers proving that not every car in the parking lot belonged to camera toting tourists. The maze of rock turned us around a little resulting in some bush whacking to find the trail, but soon enough we were headed southwest. A backcountry campsite passed us on the left as we started to descend down a series of switchbacks. The trail finally settled out into gentle rolling hills. It really felt more like an afternoon walk in the woods at home than a mountain hike. The afternoon sun was bright, and the forest had a golden hue about it that happens in the dusty dry colors of early fall. I tried to take pictures of it but of course they never turn out quite right. We picked up some gigantic acorns from a chestnut oak. My dad said he was going to plant them when we got home. We started turning a little north and although I really had no exact measure of distance on any map, it started to feel like we had gone too far. I was worried we had wandered off the main trail and were on an ATV track going who knows where. Finally, I made the old "Let's just see what is on the other side of that hill" statement which is often made in times of great doubt. That statement comes up usually after about 5 to 10 minutes of feeling that things aren't looking right. Essentially, you put a time or distance limit on your confusion. If you don't see something reassuring in _____ distance, _____ minutes, or just after that hill/curve, you will stop and backtrack until something starts looking right. I have used this technique on many trips, and more often than not it has saved me from going too far in the wrong direction. This time my patience actually saved me from wasting time by backtracking. The way we were headed surprisingly panned out. The trail we were on made a junction with an ATV trail that ran along a creek bed headed directly north. This was exactly was the waypoint we needed to see to know we were on the right path. In about 10 minutes we descended into a hollow by a cliff, and there was Windless Cave.

In the side of the cliff was a large, deep gash of an overhang, about 10 feet high and 30 yards wide. There was a dry stream bed flowing into it, leading to who knows where. I walked in as far as I dared, which wasn't that far. For some reason I didn't bring along my headlamp, which is a big faux paw on any kind of hike period, but even if I had a light, I probably wouldn't have gone much further. I am embarrassed to admit that I am not much of a spelunker. Along with all the great trails, mountains, gorges, and rivers outlined in this book, Tennessee is the home to more caves than any other state. In 2011, a statewide survey listed 9,600 caves, with over 5,700 in the northern plateau. Other than casually sticking my head inside for a quick look around, I have never really been inside a single one of them. It isn't that I have pervasive fear of enclosed spaces, but the whole idea of even temporarily questioning the way out is one of the most terrifying thoughts that I can conjure. During all of my above ground outdoor adventures, there have been countless times that I wasn't 100 percent sure where I was, but I never get really worried. The trail will come out somewhere. If you lose the trail, find some flowing water. If you are east of the Mississippi, it will either lead to the Atlantic Ocean or the Gulf of Mexico. Problem solved! But if you are unsure of your position in a cave, you have to entertain the possibility that you will never see the light of day again, which is truly horrifying.

The only caving experience I actually have is of course on the ridiculously dangerous end of the spelunking spectrum, which is cave diving. One time while I was on a scuba dive on Vortex Springs in the Florida panhandle, I somehow ended up following my friends Teddy and Brian into the cavern. I didn't even have a flashlight, I just swam between their flashlight beams and tried to not to stir up sand on the bottom or kick an eel. We got down to a depth of 86 feet and turned around after assessing our air supplies and general courage. When we got back to the surface, I decided that I had gotten my fill of cave diving. Those 10 minutes or so were plenty. Phobias aside, I know that someday I need to give some of these local caves a chance. I have also read the caves in Tennessee don't have as many eels.

Thankfully, throughout history not all people have been as shy as me about caves. In 2013, some of the oldest cave art in North America was discovered on the Plateau in Tennessee. It was dated to be 6,000 years old, although there are dozens more sites with carvings and paintings dated to be between 500 and 900 years old. Many of these sites are kept as closely held secrets in order to protect them. In fact many caves on public and private land are kept quiet by the people that know them best. Unlike other natural sites that are exposed to the outside elements, in a cave there is no weather to blow or rinse away garbage left by people. There are no temperature extremes to promote waste to decompose. In short, a few stupid people can totally trash them. Recently, there has been even more damage to the fragile cave ecosystems. Since it started to be closely studied in 2006, White Nose Syndrome is killing about a million bats a year in the eastern U.S. and Canada. It is spread by the fungus, Pseudogymnoascus destructans, that can completely eradicate a colony of hibernating bats. Research is ongoing to determine how it is spreading, but there is a prevailing theory that people and animals moving in and out of caves is contributing to the spread of the disease. As a response to this threat, Tennessee has closed access to all caves located on public land.

After retreating back into the light, we took a good snack break. It was after 4:30 p.m., and you could tell in the shadows that sunset was nearing. It didn't seem near as long on the way back, but it still took about an hour to return to the Black Mountain Loop. We headed north this time, going to the Northern Overlook. It was a similar rock formation that looked out over a small valley and another ridge line. It wasn't as dramatic as the southern overlook, but we had this one to ourselves. As we left to head back to the main trail, we saw the full moon rise above a ridge to the east. A cool wind was starting to blow with the setting sun. We made it back to the car with about 20 minutes of daylight left. We had been gone about 3 and half hours and had covered what I thought to be around a good 6 miles. We drove back to Crossville, ate a horrible dinner at the Apple Barrel, and started the long, dark drive to Fall Creek Falls.

This is a close view of the overlooks on the loop trail.

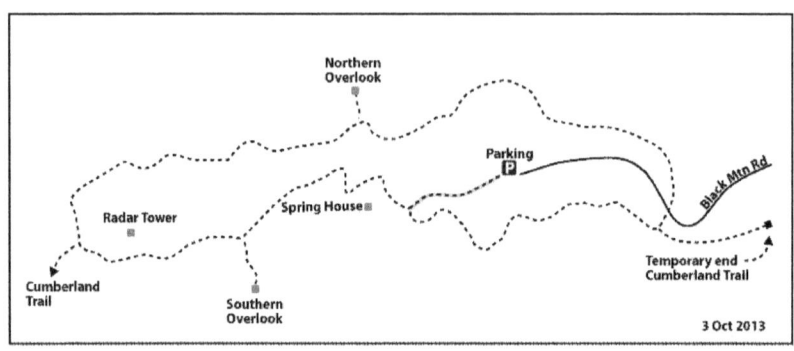

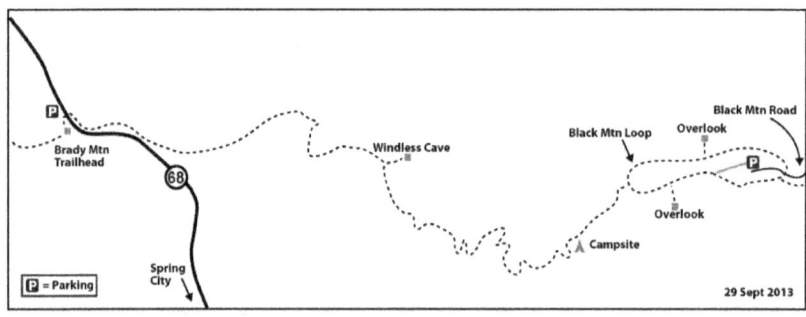

Chapter V

Fall Creek Falls State Park

If there is one place on the Cumberland Plateau that most people in this region can identify with, it is Fall Creek Falls. In fact, when trying to describe where the Plateau is to somebody, if you just say "Fall Creek Falls", they will most likely instantly get an idea of what you are talking about. Most Tennesseans, sometime in their life, have stood at the top of the Fall Creek Gorge observation deck and taken no less than 50 pictures of it. Other than the gates of Graceland and the Great Smoky Mountains National Park sign, I would imagine it is the most photographed place in the state. It is by far the most visited Tennessee State Park, with approximately 1 million visitors a year.

The park is centered around the Cane Creek gorge in the central part of the Cumberland Plateau. This area of the Plateau is south of the start of the Cumberland Mountains, and the landscape is gently rolling, with the exception of the steep gorges cut from creek drainages. The primary gorge is formed by Cane Creek, which joins Meadow Creek, Fall Creek (controlled by the dam that forms the park's lake, without the dam, Fall Creek Falls would not flow year round), Piney Creek, and Rockhouse Creek. The whole thing goes underground for a while and reemerges at a spring called Crusher Hole, then flows into the Dry Fork River, which flows into the Caney Fork, which like every other piece of flowing water in the state, eventually becomes another stupid lake (Center Hill Lake).

A typical visit to the park for most is to take a walk down to the Fall Creek Falls observation deck and have a picnic lunch. The main attraction is the name sake of the park, the 256 foot Fall Creek Falls, the highest free fall waterfall east of the Mississippi. The falls are formed by Fall Creek pouring over a semi-circle shaped sheer cliff, into a wide plunge pool. Fall creek soon joins the larger Cane Creek not far away. There is a very steep trail that leads down to the plunge pool. Of course given the amount of people, steepness of the terrain, and presence of water, there have been several deaths and serious injuries in this area. In 2010, a 2 year old was struck in the head by a falling rock from the cliffs, which may have been intentionally thrown down by kids playing above. So, be sure to take a look around for yahoos before walking under the cliff tops. There is actually plenty more to see if you are willing to put in a little work. There are five other major water falls within close proximity to the visitor center. Cane Creek Falls, Cane Creek Cascades, Rockhouse Falls, Piney Creek Falls, and Coon Creek Falls, which range in height between 45 and 250 feet and can all be easily accessed with a short day hike. There are two large cave systems, Rumbling Falls Cave and Camps Gulf Cave, which are currently closed like all other public land caves because of the spread of White Nose Syndrome among the bat population.

The story of its conservation is an odd tale. The Cane Creek watershed was barely settled, even into the early 20th century. The soil was poor for agriculture, and the mineral and timber resources were not heavily harvested due to the lack of roads and rails. Cane Creek was prone to flash floods, and a record setting flood in 1929 destroyed the few grist mills that had been built along the banks, including one that had stood above the falls since 1831. Most of the mills were never rebuilt, and the land was so eroded that farmers were eager at the opportunity to sell when the Federal government began to make purchase offers in 1937. The following year the W.P.A. and the C.C.C. began to restore the forest with the goal of establishing a new National Park. The National Park Service began park construction in 1940, but only achieved in building roads and a few parking areas before WWII stopped construction. In 1944, the National Park Service transferred Falls Creek Falls to the State of Tennessee, with the land use restricted to conservation and recreation. The State of Tennessee continued with the park building plan throughout the 1950's and 1960's, completing most of the amenities the park has today. The park ended up with a 345 acre man-made lake, a lodge with a 400 person capacity and a 5,000 square foot banquet area, 222 campsites with water and electric hookups, 30 cabins, an 18 hole golf course, and an Olympic size swimming pool. This era of park building was dominated by making State Parks a kind of one stop shop for all things family vacation. From the 1950's through the 1970's, many of Tennessee's State Parks loaded up with lodges, restaurants, and golf courses, following the same model. But as time has progressed, these facilities are becoming less and less utilized. Families simply don't vacation like that anymore. The interstates and cheap air fare allow us to get farther and farther away and the idea of week stay at a state park just does not resonate like it used to. Today, Fall Creek Falls is actually one of the few parks in the state that has been able to buck the trend. The natural beauty of the park, and its proximity to the growing metro areas of Chattanooga and Nashville, have allowed it to remain very popular. In 2014 a 1.4 million dollar renovation project was started on the lake cabins in addition to the construction of a privately operated zip line. Of course there is a good reason for the attention and money. It is consistently ranked in the top ten state parks in the nation.

I have a couple of stories about this park that are a little non-traditional. The first is a pretty boring backpacking tale, but it was special because it was the beginning of my forays on the Plateau. Like I mentioned in the intro, on Memorial Day weekend in 2002 I was looking for a good place to go backpacking that was not as far as the Smokies. Fall Creek Falls was familiar and easy to find. We originally had a big group, but in the end it wound up being my friend from college, Jerry, and my Brother in Law, Fancher. Of course, I had gotten on line and hatched a pretty ambitious plan. Imagine that.

There are really two set of hiking trails in the 26,000 acre park. There are the "Day Use" trials, which are a series of 10 trials, primarily centered around the visitor center, the lake, and the main attraction waterfalls. These trails range from 0.20 to 4.40 miles. They are heavily traveled, have a ton of interesting things to look at, and do not have any overnight campsites on them. Then there are two "Overnight Trails", one 12 mile Lower Loop, which is actually north of the visitor center, and a 13 mile Upper Loop, south of the visitor center. The Lower Loop is the difficult rated trail that follows the Cane Creek and Piney Creek gorges. There are two backcountry campsites on this trail. The Upper Loop meanders around the rolling hills above the deep gorges. It crosses Cane Creek, but there is no dramatic scenery to it. There is one campsite on the Upper Loop. The plan for our weekend was to hike them both, covering about 25 miles and hiking out Monday morning.

After spending Friday night in Murfreesboro, we drove about an hour and a half to Fall Creek Falls. We took Highway 70 through McMinnville, because we were so close to Interstate 24. For most visitors to the park using Interstate 40, you will want take exit 288 around Cookeville and head south on TN 111 which will take you most of the way there, until you turn onto 284, which bisects the park.

We immediately headed to the visitor's center to get our permits, which were only available inside. This step always makes me a little nervous. Up until recently, there were two types of back country permit stations. There were the ones that dispense the little pieces of carbon paper contained in a plastic box under a covered pavilion at the trailhead. These are my favorite. You fill one out, stick one copy through a hole in a box, put one copy on your dashboard, put one copy in the hood of your pack, and march on. Sure, a troop of 800 Boy Scouts could be ahead of you and have every site filled in whole park, but if that happens you will just have to improvise. Most importantly, you are getting in the woods. Usually the rest will take care of itself. And then there were the places where the permits were only available inside. These are the ones where you had to talk to a ranger. These are the ones where sometimes the trip got screwed up. This is where you got told that the campsites were filled or closed. This is where you got told that fires were banned. This is where you got told that trails were closed. Personally, I would much rather bumble about with plausible ignorance. Today, almost all parks in the state have gone to online only registration for backcountry permits, which is really a much better system. But for the time period of this trip, Tennessee State Parks barely had websites. So, no matter how hard you studied and planned, your whole trip could end at the ranger desk.

Of course my fears were confirmed. There had been some severe storms recently, and the Upper Loop was closed due to fallen trees. Which left us with the Lower Loop as the only one option if we wanted to do an overnight backpacking trip. The ranger suggested that we stick to the eastern side of the gorge for the hike in to avoid other groups and have the best chance of having a campsite to ourselves. With our trip mileage cut in half, here was time to spare so we spent some time along the trails near the falls. Around 11:00 a.m. we started heading north from the Nature Center. The terrain was rolling and easy. After three miles we crossed a small, nearly stagnant creek, and found the first backcountry campsite on the left side of the trail. It was 1:00 p.m. We set up our tents, started a fire, threw Fancher's hatchet at a tree stump, found a tortoise, talked until we ran out of subjects, and eventually laid our sleeping pads in the shade and took naps. I haven't had the opportunity to take many naps on backpacking trips, but they are always a nice luxury. One time on the slopes of Mt. LeConte in the Smokies, I took a nap in the late afternoon, and when I opened my eyes there was a deer standing only a few feet from my head. I stayed as still a stone until it slowly wandered out of our campsite. For my trail nap at Fall Creek Falls, I was just awoken by mosquitos.

Soon enough we had killed enough time to reach a respectable dinner time. This was early in my backpacking career, but I was already experimenting with backcountry foods that were not dehydrated bag meals. This time I brought stovetop stuffing, wild rice, and country ham. The country ham of course turned out great. The stovetop didn't fluff under the intense heat of the stove and turned into a thick, buttery soup, which was still edible. After the ham and stuffing, I didn't have room the rice. While in the process of cooking, Jerry accidently dumped his entire dehydrated chili meal on the ground. Which reminds me of another small convenience of the Plateau, which is the lack of dangerous or semi dangerous animals. If this had been in the Smokies, we would have spent thirty minutes cleaning it up and relocating the scraps. If we had been in grizzly country out west, we would have moved the entire camp. With our stomachs full, the revelry did not last long. We had not slept much the night before so after dinner we headed to bed, although it was barely dark.

In the morning we were back on the trail around 8:30 a.m. The blown down trees were obstructing the trail in this section too and we lost our way a few times, meandering around the rim of the gorge. After bushwacking back to the trail, we crossed the lower portion of the Cane Creek Gorge. It was about a 700 foot loss of elevation and then a good climb out. This was the only really steep terrain that we encountered on the entire loop. The actual creek was crossed on a long cable bridge, which are common throughout the rest of the park. After we gained the edge of the gorge again, we found a lot more blow downs, which took time to navigate. We passed through the second campsite, which was much larger than the one we spent the night in, and even had a working well pump. We tried it out. It spewed out reddish brown water, but it did work. After we started to turn south again, it started to thunder. We reached Piney Falls, where we actually saw people for the first time. After crossing Piney Creek on another long cable bridge, we ran into more groups of hikers. For the last 1.5 miles of trail before the Nature Center, the Lower Loop basically parallels the road. It started to rain so we decided to take the road back, arriving back at the vehicle around 4:00 pm. Our victory dinner consisted of steaks at Demo's in Murfreesboro. And thus ended my first adventure

41

on the Cumberland Plateau. Not exactly the newest Michael Bay film.

The truth is, if I knew as much about the Plateau as I do now, upon the news that our mileage was cut in half, I would have loaded the car back up and drove to South Cumberland or Fiery Gizzard. But in retrospect, I know it was still a good thing that we headed down that trail. Although it didn't get us the mileage and time in the woods that we were initially seeking, it still showed me enough of the country to make me want to try again. I learned that there was something really worth seeing up there, and that it was not hard to get to, which has motivated a whole lot more trips.

My second Fall Creek Falls story is about a trail race. For me, hiking will be forever tied up with running. I had only been on a couple of hiking trips with my dad before a November day in 1996 when we hiked up to the Chimney Tops (GSMNP) with my older cousin and my uncle. On the way up, my cousin, who is four years younger than me, left me in the dust as he bounded up the trail. I was 16 years old, winded and exhausted. I knew I wanted to be in the mountains more than anything, but I had to get stronger if I wanted to get very far. After we got home that next week, I was outside in the back yard and decided to see how far I could run. I ran up to the fields on the hill behind our house, across the freshly harvested soybean stalks, all the way to the highest point along a power line cut that lead to our neighbor's land. It was barely a quarter of a mile. I was winded and exhausted as I walked down. I did it the next day and ran a little further, and I kept at it until I could run the whole way up and back down. Next, I decided to see if I could run a whole mile on the road. I did it and kept going. With the exception of a few small periods of a few weeks here and there, I have ran multiple times a week for the past twenty years.

I ran a slew of 5K's, then several half marathons, and then a full marathon, until I decided to try to run a trail race for the first time. My friend Rob from Knoxville came down one October, and we drove to Montgomery Bell State Park to run the 7.6 mile Two Lakes Trail Run, which is part of the Tennessee State Parks Running Tour (which is a great source for cool races with very cheap entry fees). To train for it I tried to build a short trail through the woods on my family's land. When it came time for the race I found myself more excited than I had been for any running event in a long time. It was a perfect, cool day in mid-October, which by my definition is the finest month for running. There was a fire going in the picnic pavilion fireplace by the start line, and that first sweet smell of wood smoke in cold air hung around the check in area. The race started, and after a small section of road to allow space for the pack to thin out, we got into the woods. I have never seen 7.6 miles go by so quickly. There was a point at the end where I was totally alone, bounding down this long, gentle ridge, cool wind blowing the yellow and orange hickory and poplar leaves across the trail. I was so inspired that I actually sped up, at the end of a race! I believe that there is something innately spiritual about trail running. There is something about running through the trees that appeals to something deep in our human spirit. Humans can do a lot with our minds, but our pure animal based talent lies in running. For tens of thousands of years, the only way we hunted was to primarily run our quarry down. There are only a few animals on earth that can out run a human over distance. There is even an annual "Man versus Horse" race in Wales, and sometimes the human beats the horse. When we run in the woods, we reconnect with that part of our humanity, and it just feels right.

So after I had such a good time on the Two Lakes Trail Run, I decided to look for a little bit longer of a race. I came across the Fall Creek Falls Half Marathon. The timing of it was perfect, another October race. And this time, being on the Cumberland Plateau, the temperatures should have been even cooler for that time of year. This was 2010, and at the time it was part of the Xterra Race Series. Today, there is still a half marathon, full marathon, and 50K at Fall Creek Falls, but it not part of that series and is held in late February.

This trip began with my dad and I hiking the Grassy Cove section of the Cumberland Trail (see Chapter IV). When we finished up as the sun was sinking low on the nearby ridges, we headed to grab dinner near Crossville and drove on to Fall Creek Falls in the dark. It was 8:30 p.m. by the time was got checked in at the Lodge. There was no cell phone signal, and we called home using an actual land line phone. There was a long day heading toward me so I got to sleep as soon as possible, after watching just a little football of course. The morning broke very cold with a light frost on the roof tops and the grass. There was a thick layer of fog hanging on the lake, which could be viewed directly off our balcony. We grabbed some quick breakfast off the buffet and went back to the room for a minute before we packed up to check out. It was a little after 8:00 a.m. when we left the parking lot, heading to the race check in. There was still plenty of time so we made a quick detour to the falls observation area. It was very quiet, with only a few other people in sight. There was a thick, foggy mist clinging to the walls of the gorge. I really wanted to hike to the bottom but there was just no time for it. We drove on to the Nature Center parking area, where the check in and start line was. With the sun steadily rising above the trees now, the temperature was in the upper 40's. It was supposed to be a sunny day with temperatures near 60 degrees, after the fog burned off. I had on a hooded sweatshirt, but was going to run in a short sleeve t-shirt and shorts. The pack of about 50 other runners was dressed in an assortment of gear. Some looked like they were going day hiking, long pants, camel bak and all. Some were stripping off their shirts and pining their numbers on their shorts leg. We got our race instructions. The course was following the Upper Overnight Loop, the trail that was closed to us eight years earlier. The 9:00 a.m. start time came, and I handed my sweatshirt to my dad and walked up the hill toward the start line. Then of course I stood around shivering, which is how all good races have to start. Finally the bullhorn tone went off and we got to moving. We followed a gravel road for a half mile or so until the pack settled down into a thin column, then we entered the woods.

After about another half mile I found a pretty good group of three to pace off of. Just like road races, finding a good pace group is important on trail runs, but the great thing about trial runs is that it is much easier to keep track of your pacers because the pack is so narrow. I knew I was going to be ok when I looked at my watch. I had been running for 40 minutes, and I felt like it had only been 10 minutes. I eventually passed one of the runners in the group and stayed behind a couple wearing trail running gaiters. They looked pretty serious. It is always a risky proposition to make pacing judgments based on how a runner is dressed, but this time it worked out for me. The three of us passed several other groups and individuals, but I never had any problems keeping up. Most of our passing happened on hill stretches when others stopped to walk up. This trail was very gently rolling, with the largest elevation swings between 150 and 200 feet. There were a lot of briars, but I was able to keep an eye out for them and miss them when I could. We crossed a lot of dry creek beds, and the trail conditions were dry and fast. I stayed right with my gaiter friends until the trail broke out on the road, half a mile from the finish line. I knew the end was near, and I felt like I still had plenty in the tank. I never want to finish with plenty in the tank. I started a downhill stretch and turned it on, passing my two gaiter wearing pacers. I saw my dad near the finish line with a camera. As I strode through the finish line I heard my time called out, 2:13:40. I couldn't believe I had done that well, but my watch confirmed it too. What can I say? I was born and raised in a briar patch.

The Lower Loop is the long trail that leads north from the Nature Center and crosses Cane Creek Gorge before turning back south, crossing Piney Creek. The Upper Loop makes a long eastern route into the rolling hills and follows Cane Creek back towards the Nature Center.

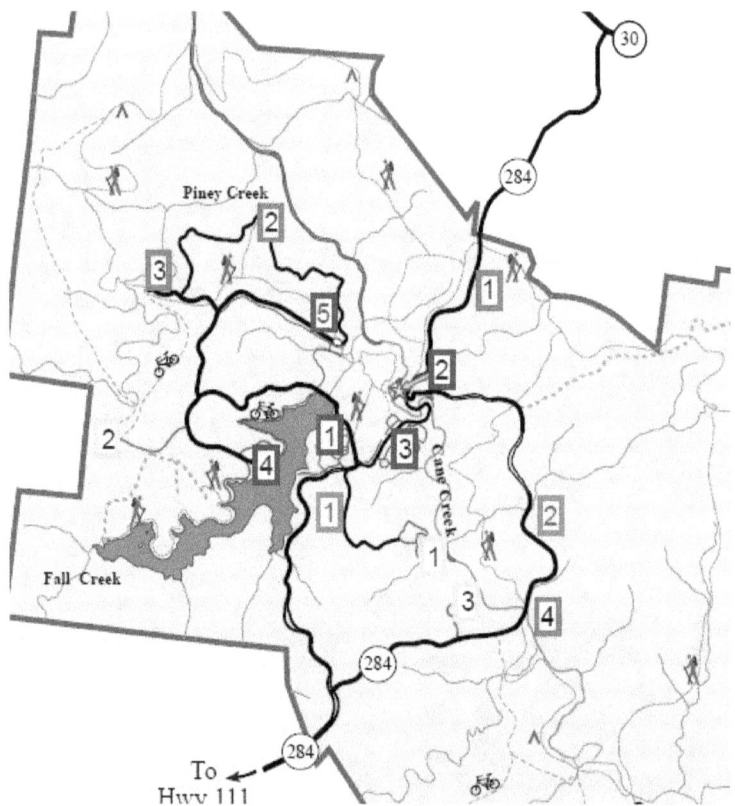

Chapter VI

South Cumberland – Savage Gulf and Stone Door

This chapter is the most extensive undertaking in this book due to the mileage and variety of trips that I am trying to cover. South Cumberland State Park is not a traditionally shaped park. It is actually a collection of nine geographically separate areas spread throughout Grundy, Franklin, Marion, and Sequatchie Counties. The largest sections, Savage Gulf and Stone Door, are considered two separate "areas" in the park, however they are the only two that are contiguous and share a trail system. Their combined presence occupies 15,900 acres of the total 25,539 acres of South Cumberland. The other significant part of South Cumberland is Fiery Gizzard which is has its own chapter in this book.

Just like the Cumberland Trail, South Cumberland has its own established fan base and supporters. I would highly encourage visiting the Friends of South Cumberland website at www.friendsofscsra.org before you take a trip, at minimum to learn about the latest trail news. You can also join a "meet up" group, learn about upcoming events at the park, print off maps, and even shop for some South Cumberland related merchandise. Of course you can donate to the preservation of the park as well as volunteer. There are very nice detailed topographical maps available at the ranger stations (and for purchase on the Friends' website); however for ease of reading I used the simplified trail map for this chapter.

This park is far and above the "biggest bang for your buck" hiking place I have ever visited. It is difficult to hike more than a mile without seeing either an overlook or a waterfall. Compared to many Smokies hikes where you can easily hike a loop of over 10 miles to see one feature, at Savage Gulf/ Stone Door you essentially have so many things to look at that many of them get bypassed due to time restrictions. I have taken many people here on their first backpacking trip because I know at least they will see plenty to keep them motivated. That being said, you still earn it here. There are trails along the rims that are pretty fast, flat, and full of more overlooks than you have time to see, but anything that descends into the gorge and follows one of the drainages will eventually turn into a steep series of boulder steps. There are some stretches of boulder fields on the walls of the gorges where the trail is difficult to follow, and I really would try to avoid hiking at night. The whole park is centered around streams so water sources are plentiful, and the backcountry campsites are good size with most having vault toilets. There is one important point about the water sources though. Don't walk on a trail beside a creek or stream and assume you will always have a water source at hand as long as you stay in the drainage area. Almost all water sources here will disappear underground at some point. Most will come back to the surface eventually.

However; I do have to mention one drawback of this park. All of those great aspects that I mentioned above, those are not secrets. When I first took my first trip there about 14 years ago, we went to Hobbs cabin on a sunny Saturday afternoon in the summer. We saw two other hikers. Today, on a typical Saturday morning people start hiking at daylight along the fastest possible route to claim the best campsites by 9:00 a.m. If you show up to the parking lot much after 9:00 a.m., you will be parking on the road. As the population of Middle Tennessee has boomed in the last decade, so has the popularity of backpacking, and Savage Gulf/Stone Door is 90 minutes away from most of metro Nashville. My stories involve getting backcountry permits from the trail kiosks as we pulled into the parking lot. This process was changed in 2015. Now all permits have to be obtained on-line, and there is a $6 charge. This was bound to happen. There was no way it could continue on the way it was. On my last few trips there have had to be rangers in the campsites sorting out the chaos. I hate to see the fee, but it is less than most fast food meals, and at least it is going to a good cause.

My personal story with this park began in July of 2003. I was trying to get a short trip together and batted around the idea of going back to Fall Creek Falls, only to find out that essentially all of the trails were closed. I started to look around the state map again and spotted the Stone Door and Savage Gulf swath of green. I had never been there, but I remembered my parents talking about a visit they had and how they had seen backpackers. There was essentially no information on the internet, just some directions to the ranger stations and a phone number. I called the number and asked if you could do any backpacking there. I will never forget the answer from the ranger, "Son, that is all there is to do here!" I could hardly believe my luck. I had found a new favorite place.

Savage Gulf and Stone Door form the shape of a giant crow's foot in the Plateau. The three "claws" are three gorges are formed by Big Creek, Savage Creek, and the Collins River, which continues to flow north forming the base of the "foot". There are 55 miles of hiking trials, and I have been on most of them. I arranged this chapter in three loops, one for each gorge. The following hikes are arranged west to east, but you could easily mix and shuffle them because all of the gorges are connected by trails. Trips here could range between a short overnighter to the better part of a week. Each of the hiking loops I describe starts from a different Ranger Station or parking area. I made an attempt to describe directions but I heavily encourage the use of Google Maps in this area.

Stone Door Loop

This 10.2 mile hike was my first experience in the Stone Door area. In early November I met my friend Rob at the Stone Door Ranger Station parking lot around 9:00 a.m. Coming from the west, the best way to get there is take I-24 to the Pelham exit (127) and go east on State Route 50. Follow it to Altamont, veer north on State Route 56, follow to Beersheba Springs, and take Stone Door Road on your right. These towns are about as big as they sound so if you blink you will miss them. We started down the Stone Door Trail, following it 0.9 mile to the Big Creek Gulf Trail. It was perfect weather, sunny with highs in the 60's and lows in the 40's. The trees were a little past peak but still had plenty of leaves to add some nice color to the overlooks. We crossed through the Stone Door very close to the trailhead. It is a crack 10 feet wide and 100 feet deep in the bluffs at the edge of Big Creek Gorge. It was used as a passage way by Native Americans to get underneath the sheer bluffs and reach the more gentle slopes of the gorge. There is a steep stone staircase leading down the crack. It is a pretty easy walk, but I wouldn't want to tumble down it. That morning we passed several Boy Scout groups rappelling off the cliffs. After the stone steps it was typical switchbacks to the bottom of the gorge and the junction with the Big Creek Gulf Trail.

After 1.1 miles on the Big Creek Gulf Trial, there is a spur trial to Ranger Falls on the left. It is a 0.4 mile boulder hop, and we wisely dropped our packs at the junction. Ranger Falls is a nice waterfall, but compared to most of the other falls in the park it is a little on the short side. The creek tumbles off a pretty wide shelf into a shallow plunge pool which is also a "sinks". Sinks, which are very common in this park, are places where water sources disappear underground. It is all part of the crazy, intricate subterranean system of caves that exists under the Plateau. We ate an early lunch at the base of the falls and headed back to the main trail. We followed Big Creek Gulf Trail another 2 miles as it climbed out of the gorge to the Alum Gap Campsite, which is also at the junction of Big Creek Rim Trail. It was early in the afternoon, barely after 1:00 p.m. on a Saturday, but there were only a few sites left. There were no sites left near the cliff tops. We grabbed one that looked pretty decent and set up our tent to officially stake our claim. Getting to camp this early was part of the plan. We grabbed our daypacks and headed down the 1.4 mile long Greeter Trail to Greeter Falls.

On the way we passed Broadtree falls, but the Broadtree Branch creek was barely flowing with the dry fall weather, and we peered at the trickle over the 30 feet of stacked sedimentary rocks. We ended up walking down the steep trail to the bottom but did not linger too long and climbed back up the main trail to proceed to Greeter. The Greeter Trail ends at the Greeter Falls, with the high trail going to Upper Greeter Falls and a spur descending to the base of Lower Greeter Falls. Upper Greeter is where Firescald Creek takes a wide drop over a long, short sheer bluff, with a giant boulder dividing the flow in the middle of the falls. Lower Greeter is where the creek is consolidated into a narrower flow and plunges fifty feet over a second sheer bluff into a plunge pool surrounded by large slab boulders. The trail to the base of the falls actually follows a metal spiral staircase down the side of the cliffs. A wooden staircase and bridge plank leads to the large boulders at the end of the plunge pool. If it had been summer it would have been a great place to swim. We scrambled along the rocks and took some pictures. It was still mid-afternoon, but we knew the November sun was starting to set quicker every day, and we wanted to have plenty of time to cook in the daylight. We trekked back up the stairs to the main trail and headed back toward the campsite.

It was around 4:00 p.m. when we got back to camp. We had barely reached our site when a small group of four hikers, three women and one man, wandered down the campsite connector trail nearest us. These trails spread like a spider web all over the campsite area, connecting the individual spots to the main trail junction. They asked us if we knew of any empty sites. We sent them back toward the privy, where I had notice some empty spaces earlier, but they soon came back saying that there were no sites left. They didn't look like complete psycho killers so we invited them to share our site. We only had one tent and there was plenty of room anyway. It was a pretty eclectic group that had arranged themselves on one of those "meet up" websites that organize hikes. One of the women was a National Park Service Ranger. She was only seasonal, playing the ranger game of working part time at far flung parks while trying to score a permanent position, and then an eventual transfer to a "G" or "Y" park (Great Smoky Mountains, Glacier, Grand Canyon, Yellowstone, and Yosemite). Another had recently come back from traveling in "Georgia the Country". She said it like that several times, and I totally understood because there is a big difference between going to a University of Georgia football game in Athens versus touring around a remote former Soviet Republic that is currently kind of in a war with Russia. I would call it "Georgia the Country" as well. She had also used a couch surfing website to travel through Europe, sleeping on random people's couches for a single night and moving on. And she accomplished this apparently without being chopped into pieces and becoming the story line for Hostel 4. I never got much of a back story on the man, except that he was trying use the wisp of cell phone signal available to post to social media, and he hiked barefooted. I am not kidding. He actually freaking did it. He was wearing shoes in camp but I witnessed him doing it the next morning.

I got a fire started, and Rob and I started on our planned dinner of chicken alfredo. In 1999, I went on my first backpacking trip and ate my first de-hydrated bag meal. After I realized that the gumbo tasted an awful lot like the chili which tasted an awful lot like the chicken and wild rice, I secretly devoted myself to finding better backcountry fare. I have had some really bad misses, like trying to make cornbread, but I have had some decent successes too. My best successes have been with pasta dishes. The main obstacle with pasta dishes is of course the sauce issue. You realistically can't easily carry a glass jar of pasta sauce, so I have tried various powdered sauces that come in little paper pouches. The catch about these sauce pouches is that you have to pay attention to the directions. The preparation cannot be too dependent upon adding milk or butter, both in pretty short supply in the woods. So you have to figure a way to pull it off using mainly water. This particular time, I packed in a pouch of chunked chicken breast. We used some of the pasta water and some of the chicken stock from the package to make the sauce as we stirred in the alfredo powder. I also brought along some grated parmesan and some crushed red pepper. It worked. I have paid $30 for much worse meals at the Olive Garden. We couldn't finish it all we shared it with our new friends, who were impressed and eager to supplement their bag meal chili/gumbo/wild rice they had brought along. We finished eating just as the last of the sinking sun was filtering through the trees. Which is perfect timing because I hate eating with a head lamp.

In general, I have always been hesitant to embrace the whole trail camaraderie aspect of hiking. I am not explicitly anti-social in the woods, but I have never been one to seek out the company of other hikers. I will always speak to folks and maybe share some chit chat about the weather or trail conditions, but typically a few minutes of interaction is sufficient for me. Of course there are some times you share a shelter with another group and get into long drawn out conversations that stretch for hours, but for the most part I really want my wilderness experiences to be shared with the people I choose to take the trip with. Besides, you can meet some real weirdoes out there and escape is not always easy. However; I will admit this particular instance was actually enjoyable. We all stayed up late, telling stories by the fire, mostly full of the typical hiker dribble that would bore most normal humans to tears. Only hikers keep other hikers captivated for hours with detailed discussions of their personal theories on footwear and goose down.

The night got down in the low 40's, so it was pretty cool by the time I crawled into our tent. One thing I have found in my outdoor adventures is that no matter how experienced you think you are, you are still capable of making bad decisions with your gear. For some reason, be it the warm late October days we had experienced, or just that I was trying to save weight in my pack after loading that package of chicken and large cooking pot, I had opted to bring my light, fleece, summer sleeping bag. I also brought my down jacket with the intention of wearing it in my sleeping bag, essentially turning it into a cold weather bag. Not soon after laying down I realized that my plan was going to work, for at least half of my body. My legs and feet were freezing all night, but I was able to halfway sleep decently.

Not surprisingly I was the first one up in the morning. I grabbed my camera and wandered through the briars and undergrowth around our campsite to the thinly spread pines along the edge of the bluff. The sun was just rising over the eastern rim of the Big Creek Gorge. The bottom of the gorge was about 700 feet below. The trees seemed to have lost more leaves over night, but really things just look different at long distances in the bright morning light. One of out of five trees still had an orange canopy, which seemed to be equally distributed along the sides of the gorge. The rest of the trees were winter barren. Of course the bluff tops were covered in Loblolly Pines.

The Loblolly, or *Pinus Taeda*, is a scraggly branched, southern yellow conifer whose natural range was primarily located in the deep southern states. Due to its ability to grow quickly in varied environments and soil conditions, as well as the commercial value of its timber which is used for construction materials, the Loblolly has been transplanted all over the United States. It is now the second most common tree in our nation, only behind the red maple. These particular Loblollies in the park most likely came from the reclamation of the clear cut forests, harvested before the park was established. Loblollies were also heavily planted by the C.C.C. in the 1930's for erosion control. Of course, now we understand that when you replace an indigenous hardwood forest full of biodiversity with neatly placed rows of quick growing pine trees, you really haven't really fixed what was messed up. Today, conservation practices involve actually replacing the kind of trees that were initially cut down, but these stands of Loblollies still cover the landscape as a reminder of a time when we first started to pay attention to how screwed up we had made things. I don't try to look too despairingly upon the scraggly Loblolly. A tree is still a tree.

I took some pictures of the sunrise, and soon Rob joined me. We took turns taking heavily posed pictures on the edge of the cliff top. We wandered back to camp as our campsite mates were stirring. We cooked breakfast and packed independently but somehow wound up ready to hit the trail at the same time. It was 3.2 miles along the Big Creek Rim Trail to the junction with the Stone Door Trail. All of the rim trails in this park are pretty similar. They are mostly flat and very fast. The only thing that slows you down is stopping to enjoy the overlooks that occur at nearly 100 yard or less intervals along the sheer bluff that caps the rim of the gorge. We ended up staying with the other group pretty much the whole way out. We continued our friendly conversation and continued to observe the barefoot guy. It was a cold morning and the trail was rocky and covered in pine cones, but he just motored along like he was wearing a broken in pair of Merrells. He didn't even look down at where he was stepping. His pace was completely normal. It was astounding.

The wind was blowing hard with an approaching cold front, causing a blizzard of leaves to swirl around us whenever the trail ventured deeper into the trees. At one of the last overlooks we looked down the rim and saw the crowd gathered at the end of the Stone Door. We picked our way through the crowd without stopping and climbed the Stone Door Trail again. In 0.9 miles we were back to the Ranger Station. We said goodbye to our friends and used the weak phone signal to check the scores from the football games we had missed on Saturday. Things had not turned out well for our beloved Volunteers in their game against Missouri. We had been much better off in the woods than we would have been cussing in front of a TV.

Collins West to Sawmill Loop

This is the 13 mile loop of 13 mile loops, the hike of hikes. Of all the trips described in this book, I have by far the most experience over this little stretch of ground. I have carried nearly a dozen people on their first backpacking trip along this loop. It has everything you could ask for in a neat little package perfect for single overnighter, or it could be stretched into two nights if you don't start until later in the afternoon. There are two nice waterfalls, a nice rock hop stream crossing across a huge sinks, a boulder field crossing, an unusual water source, plenty of nice overlooks, some nice steep switchbacks, and two nice large backcountry campsites. And there is one other little detail that makes this a great first trip, which I usually don't disclose to the hiking rookies before we start. Because you start the trip with a descent, like most trips on the Plateau, the really drawn out hard stuff doesn't start until the second day. You are at the bottom of the gorge, and there is only one way to get home, which is up and out. Quitting is not an option. I have made the mistake of taking first timers on trips in the Smokies which typically begin with a 6 to 8 mile uphill slog, whereupon I find myself giving a perpetual motivational pep talk for most of the first day. I have never had anyone quit, but I have seen some come close. But if you put them at the bottom of a gorge, with only means of escape being four miles of switchbacks, a person will always find their motivation.

I have done this loop so many times that I am not going to pick a particular trip in which to frame the story. Although, I would like to say that I first did this hike with my dad, when he accompanied me on his first backpacking trip. It was March of 2004, and somehow or another, I have done almost all the proceeding trips in March and April as well. After my first trip to the park the previous year and the long flat loop to Hobbs Cabin, I wanted to really go down in one of the gorges and get a closer look at what we had been seeing at from those overlooks near Hobbs. This loop stood out easily as the north/south loop which covers the whole of the Collins River Gulf (or gorge), which is the middle "claw" of the crow's foot. It follows the entire length of the Collins Gulf Trail as well as the Stagecoach Historic Trail.

The trailhead for this journey begins at Collins West Access. This is not a ranger station, just a parking lot with a trailhead. If you are coming from I-24, take State Route 50 to Altamont, but instead of taking Highway 56 north, like for Stone Door, you take it south, down to the junction with Highway 108. Turn left, following 108 going east, to Gruetli-Laager, and then take 55th Avenue on your left going north until there is no more road. From the parking lot, you are going to head out on the only trailhead, but you will quickly come to an intersection with Collins Gulf Trail. It is important to mention here that the detailed map you get at the ranger station describes this trail very well, but the beginning it references is the Stagecoach Historic Trail and the end it references is Sawmill Campground. This loop actually starts in the middle of this long trail.

At the intersection, which is well marked like all trails are in this park, go east, towards Collins East. The trail will turn south and descend quite steeply, almost seeming like a staircase, until it levels off and begins to ramble through a boulder field for several hundred yards. These boulder fields are found all over the Plateau, but in my experience, this particular one is the longest that I have ever encountered. What is a boulder field? Well, most of the gorges or gulfs on the Plateau follow a pretty standard pattern. The rims are sandstone bluffs that stand 50 to 100 feet high. Below them there is a steep slope that slowly eases in steepness until the river bed or creek bed is reached. However; occasionally the sides of the gorge are so steep that erosion eventually causes them to tumble down, strewing car size boulders along the bottom stretch of the slope. On this particular stretch, the trail meanders up and over these boulders on a track that is sometimes hard to follow. As long as you keep the white trail blazes in sight you will stay in the right direction. Soon the trail turns back into a normal path, and a bridge crossing the Collins River will appear on your left. It is very well constructed bridge, as all the bridges in the park are. The Collins River is roaring underneath you as you pause in the middle of the bridge to take a few pictures. Enjoy it while you have the chance, it soon goes underground, and you will only be looking at a dry river bed at further crossings to the north. At this point, between the long descent and the boulder field navigation, you will feel like you have made a lot of progress, but it has only been 1.1 miles since the parking lot. There is a lot more ground to cover. Within another 0.4 mile you will reach Collins East campsite. I have stayed here before when I got started in the mid-afternoon and turned the loop into a two night trip. This is a good campsite, flat and wide, but you will have to go back towards the Collins River for water.

Continuing on, now winding north along the eastern rim of the Collins River Gorge, the walking now is relatively easy and flat. There are occasionally some small streams to cross, but they are navigated with quick rock hops. There are plenty of overlooks, such as Collins River Overlook, Standing Rock Overlook, Horsepound Overlook, and Blue Branch Overlook. There are many more that are not named. Any of these is a great spot for lunch. There are enough overlooks that you will be able to try out some of your orienteering skills if you have the detailed topographic map. By looking across to curves and ridges on the opposite side of the gorge, and by watching the stream crossings, you can judge your location pretty accurately.

Along this stretch of trail, you will encounter a sight that I personally have had the fortune to never witness in any other park that I have ever visited. There are short stretches that essentially follow the edge of the park boundary. These sections give you a commanding view of the devastation that has befell the unprotected wilderness. The timber companies are very efficient, and clear cut right to the edge of the park. After walking for hours in dense forest you come upon a landscape that looks like it was used as an aerial bombing test range. Everything is flattened as far as you can see, with the earth covered in a thick, impenetrable tangle of dead branches and tree stumps. Suddenly, you will find yourself very grateful for every effort made and dollar spent on this park, because you know what it would look like if not for some dedicated individuals.

When most people think of agriculture in the Southeastern U.S., they think of cotton, tobacco, corn, rice, and soybeans. And while it is true that the fertile river valleys and river bottoms are heavily utilized for row crops, people often do not know that the other great southern agriculture product is timber, which comes from pretty much everywhere else that doesn't have a building on it. The Southeast, unlike the Pacific Northwest or The Great North Woods, rarely has harsh winter weather and stays relatively warm and sunny. Combine those attributes with our abundance of precipitation, and you have the perfect weather for tree growing. Combine the perfect weather for tree growing with a well-developed transportation system and an abundant work force, and you get the perfect place for tree harvesting. Over 55 percent by volume of the U.S. timber harvest comes from the Southeast (sometimes nicknamed the nation's timber basket). While this region only has 2 percent of the Earth's forest cover, it produces 25 percent of the world's pulpwood and 18 percent of the world's industrial timber.

Historically, the land was cleared for farming with the first European settlers, but in the 1880's the large timber companies discovered the South. After they had clear cut most of the timber around the Great Lakes, the Southern forest provided the next great frontier in logging. Over the next five decades almost every vestige of remaining virgin forest was logged out. Approximately 40 percent of the forest that once covered the South from the coasts to the Mississippi Delta was now leveled. The millions of tourists that flock to the Great Smoky Mountains National Park each year, stand at the overlooks at Newfound Gap, and look out over the seemingly endless landscape of forested mountains, could most likely never imagine that when the 522,419 acre park was established, only 20 percent of it still had trees. In June of 1934, the saws ran until the last minute they were legal.

Long story short, being a tree in the late 19th and early 20th century was a risky undertaking. Walking around the South today, it doesn't take long to notice that most of the trees are really young. This is astounding when you think of how old some of our forest actually were before they were destroyed. One of the famous "Daniel Boone Trees" near Blountsville, Tennessee, which bore the inscription "D. Boone Cilled A Bar On Tree In Year 1760", fell on its own in 1916. This American Beech was 28.5 feet around and approximately 365 years old, which meant that when Daniel Boone "cilled a bar" on it, the tree had been there over 200 years. The Tulip Poplar, one of my favorites and the official State Tree of Tennessee, can live for 500 years and grow 170 feet tall. White Oaks, whose natural oils allow Tennessee Whiskey and Kentucky Bourbon to age deliciously, have been documented to live 600 years. Of course, these are really just scientific and historical facts that are nearly impossible to witness in modern time. Today, to actually find trees older than 100 years, you pretty much need to leave the woods entirely. Old residential neighborhoods, church properties, and college campuses still contain some old large monoliths. But another big tree sanctuary often over looked is the cemetery. Because no matter how valuable the timber might be, nobody is logging over graves.

On the trail, the miles will wear on and you will be eagerly wanting to find the junction with the Stagecoach Historic Trail. In total it is 6.5 miles from the parking lot trailhead. On most of my overnighter loops here we reached this junction around mid-afternoon. There is a good stream here if you need to top off your water. You are about 2 miles from Sawmill Campground at this point, and it is easy to think it will be a simple downhill stretch. Well, it will be all downhill but it will not be easy.

Stagecoach Historic Trail follows an old stagecoach road that was built in the 1840's to connect McMinnville to Chattanooga. When you are descending it, it is hard to imagine that any type of wheeled vehicle could make it 100 feet, much less all the way up the gorge. The retaining walls are still standing in some spots, but the trail is a washed out mess of switchbacks full of large, loose rocks. On some stretches your best bet is to walk on the very edge and try to pick your way along to keep from having to get down into the washed area. Although this entire trial is only 1.6 miles, after 6 miles of decent hiking, this downhill trudge will beat you up in your afternoon weariness. If you can divert your eyes for a moment or two, there is plenty to look at. The trail will often cross a stream that will turn into a waterfall, then disappear underground, go underneath the trail, then reappear as another waterfall on the next set of switchbacks. About halfway down you might be able to smell campfires from Sawmill and hear voices below. Stay at it and you will eventually come to the junction with the Connector Trail. Sawmill is just 0.4 mile away. I have heard a lot of demoralized groans at this point, but the hiking will be much easier now. The bottom of the gorge will almost have a swampy feel about it as you cross cane thickets. Before you know it the smoke smell gets stronger, and the voices echo louder. You have arrived at camp!

Sawmill back country campsite pretty much sits as in the middle of the park as you can possibly get. It sits at the junction of the three gorges, right in the middle of the crow's foot. Even though Big Creek and Savage Creek gorges are close, you really only see the Collins River bed from the campsite. I say it is the Collins River bed, because you don't actually see any water here. There are the signs of a big river, a huge jumble of boulders devoid of vegetation in a swath at least thirty yards wide. There are signs of raging water, with log jams on the high sides of the bank, and debris plastered high up on near tree trunks, but I have never seen water flowing through it. The river typically stays underground although it obviously rises up in times of heavy rain. I could not imagine the power of it after a flash flood. In fact I could not imagine what the rest of the park would be like in a flash flood. It would be an impassable nightmare of deadly stream crossings. If you are ever down one of the gorges in a heavy and prolonged rain, I suggest you climb as fast as you can as quick as you can. Once you are on the top of the Plateau, you will eventually be able to find a road again and hitchhike back to your car. Don't risk your life trying to complete a loop.

The campsite, like most others in the park, has plentiful sites and a privy. It is flat with a web of trails that connects the numbered sites. The first time I was here with my dad, we pretty much had the place to ourselves. The last time I was down there (about ten years later), a team of rangers had to roam around to sort out conflicts over places to set up tents. The official water source is Schwoon Springs, which as water sources go, is pretty special. About half a mile further down the Collins Gulf trail, there is a spur trail that crosses to the west side of the Collins River bed and climbs up a slope to a 120 foot tall bluff that contains a cave and a half subterranean waterfall. The trail goes to the edge of a sinkhole where the water is spraying out of the bluff. You have to climb down to a ledge and filter the water before it flows underground. This is a real neat place, but if you can find water a little closer to camp I would take advantage of it. On some trips I have found water in pools in the river bed closer to camp. After a long day, any kind of shortening of the water getting trip will be very much appreciated. You can always drop your packs at the spur on the hike out the next morning to take a look at Schwoon.

The aggregate mileage the next day is relatively short, just about 4 miles to the parking lot, but between stops for waterfall viewing and a long hard set of switchbacks, it will seem like a lot longer distance. I would almost allow between three to four hours to be on the safe side. Follow the

Collins Gulf Trail south now, past the Schwoon Springs spur, and you will cross a bridge across the dry river bed, which I assume must have water often enough to warrant the bridge. One mile later, 1.5 miles after leaving camp, you will arrive at Fall Creek Sinks. This area is a convergence of a couple of small streams that disappear into a cave not long after crossing the trail. This is the most technical rock hop of the trip by far. On my first backpacking trip ever, which was a winter trip in the Smokies, we went down this ridiculous trail with over fifteen stream crossings. On the last stream crossing, I fell face first into a deep flowing current and became completely submerged in the near freezing water. Since then I have developed a slight phobia of stream crossings. For a while it was really bad. I would get on a slick rock in the middle of a stream, start to feel uneasy, and just jump into the water and wade out, cussing louder with each step. I just had no confidence that my next step would not send me head first into some raging stream, head over heels, arms wildly flailing. Now, years later, after many hours of therapeutic rock hops, I am better. Although I do get plenty nervous around the really slick, mossy stuff. However; that being said, this crossing of Fall Creek should be no problem for those lacking the psychological baggage that I have.

After Fall Creek Sinks, the trail continues to climb slightly, and in 0.3 miles there is a spur on the left that will take you down a very steep track to Horsepound Falls. Drop your packs here and grab some food and water for your mid-morning snack, this is the best place you are going to find. Slide down the trail to the rocks at the edge of top of the falls, which is a wide plunge off a 20 foot tall sheer bluff. Take a good rest here because you are about to have to get to work. You have covered about half of the hike out, and not gained much in elevation. After Horsepound, the trail begins to really climb. First it just climbs higher and higher from the Collins River Bed. Then it begins some honest switchbacks that work up to the edge of the bluff that forms the top of the western rim. This is some serious hiking, but really doesn't last very long. I already mentioned that for some reason I have always done this section in early spring, which is a season that always contains some very deceptive temperatures. It is hard to understand unless you have really experienced it, but a sunny day in the high 60's in late March, is significantly warmer than an 80 degree day in April. In late March there are still no leaves on the trees, and every ounce of sunshine pounds down around you and radiates off the rocks and the dry leaves. I have had some hot hikes up this section and have been very grateful for every ounce of water I filtered out of Schwoon Springs.

Once you near the rim of the gorge, the trail follows some pretty narrow paths through the rocks along the edge of the bluff. Overlooks are plentiful. Soon you turn away from the Collins Gorge, enter the Rocky Mountain Creek drainage, and see your last major landmark of the voyage, Suter Falls. You approach the shower like falls from its base, in a large hollowed out basin of rocky scree. A small bridge crosses the creek, and the trail angles up the rocky slope. It is less than 0.5 mile to the parking lot now, but the trial will still make you work for it, not leveling off until you reach the junction that you saw the previous day. This time you will head towards Collins West, and the parking lot will soon emerge through the trees. You made it!

Savage Ranger Station to Hobbs Cabin Loop

This 20 mile loop starts from the Savage Gulf Ranger Station. The access is off Highway 108, the same road that you turn off to access Collins West. This time take State Route 399, north off Highway 108, and you will dead end directly at the Ranger Station parking area.

Hobbs Cabin was a part of the first hike that I ever went on in South Cumberland. It was just my friend Jerry that made that first trip with me. Knowing what I know now, it wasn't a very imaginative hike that we planned out, but at the time it was really the best we could do. There was very limited information on the internet, and the only directions I had ended up taking us right to the Savage Gulf Ranger Station. I didn't know about the Stone Door and Collins West accesses. We also had no map in advance, so we literally planned our hike while standing at the ranger's desk and getting our backcountry permits. Hobbs Cabin Campground seemed like a good distance away, 8.5 miles, and the route hugged the northern rim of the Savage Creek Gorge. It was going to be an out and back hike. We followed the North Rim, which is like all other rim trials in the park, fast and full of overlooks. This was my first look ever at the "gulfs" of Savage Gulf, and I was impressed at the constant vistas and ruggedness of the terrain. We got to Hobb's Cabin campsite early in the afternoon. The campsite is relatively flat and full of sites. Of course the small cabin is the most coveted one. It is a good sized backpacking shelter, as far as shelters go. The wooden floor is elevated on stone foundation piers, and the tin roof extends over a small porch. Inside there is a stone fireplace, a table with a bench along one wall, and two sets of three bunk sleeping shelves along the other two walls. The max occupancy would be six, unless some wanted to sleep on the floor. We checked it out and found it was already full of people. They had a fire going in the fireplace. It was June, and I almost choked from the heat just by walking past the doorway and looking in. They were sitting on the bunk shelves in the dark, stuffy, heat and staring at each other. There was one small window, covered by a screen, but it let in very little light. Even if the place had been empty, we still wouldn't have stayed there.

The rest of the campsite was empty and we found a spot near a small stream and refilled our water for the evening. That night, this guy who said he was hiking by himself, came over and joined our fire. He said that he worked for Averitt Express. He kept making these vague references to drugs, like he was wanting us to chime in somehow. I thought he was either a cop or a drug dealer or a drug dealing cop. After 30 minutes of very awkward conversation, he shuffled on. After all these years, I still think of that weird guy every time I see an Averitt Express truck.

In the morning we awoke to a beautiful June day. We hiked out fast, but still took our time on the overlooks, seeing essentially no one the entire way. Ten years later, on a cold November morning, I ran into at least 50 other hikers on the exact same stretch, all bound to be the first to claim the cabin.

That was a fun hike, but there is a pretty decent loop that will vary up the terrain and give you a shot at the cabin as well. The crew on this hike in November of 2014 was Jack and Rob. It was easy for me to pick the route on this one, it was the last part of the "crow's foot" that I had not traveled. This most eastern gorge in the park is part of the Savage Creek drainage, which converges with the Collins River near the Sawmill Campsite, which is typically flowing underground, of course.

We set out a little before 10:00 a.m. and followed the Savage Day Loop Trail for 1.2 miles until the junction with the South Rim Trail. The weather was perfect backpacking weather, high of 50 degrees, meaning you could wear short sleeves and never break much of a sweat. We crossed a suspension bridge across Savage Creek, and after 0.5 mile we came to the Savage Falls overlook. We continued to make great time along the South Rim Trail, which was fast and full of overlooks. Around lunch time we stopped at Laurel Bluff overlook for a long break, which was one of the widest overlooks in this part of the park. The trail started to turn south and began to descend. Soon I saw the familiar junction of the Stagecoach Historic Trail and the Collins Gulf Trail.

I think I first began to worry about time when we reached this junction. It was a place that I had seen many times, coming from the Collins Gulf Trail, and I recognized it instantly. Now we had to descend the Stagecoach Historic to reach the junction with the Connector. I also remembered all the times I had gone down that trail on the way to Sawmill Campsite and how rough those little 1.6 miles are and how they seem to drag on. It was getting on 2:00 p.m. We had covered 7 miles so far (5.8 miles on Collins Gulf and 1.2 on Savage Day Loop), but we still had a long way to go, and the November afternoons go quick. There was no time to talk about it too much, we just dove into the 1.6 mile, slidey, rocky trail ahead. We had only seen a couple other people on the trail that morning. From this point, we would not see another hiker until the next morning.

It was 3:00 p.m. we started on the Connector Trail. I had no illusions about what we were getting into. There was no way we were going to avoid some night time hiking. Now, in the bottom of the gulfs, it was almost seeming dusk-like, and the sun was hovering closer and closer to the western rim. Still, looking back on it, I don't think that we messed around a lot and wasted time. I suppose we could have moved on the South Rim trail a little faster, but ultimately, it was just a lot of mileage to tackle with a mid-morning start in November daylight. Of course compounding my worries was that not only were we going to run out of daylight, but we were going to run out of daylight on what was supposed to be the hardest trail in the park, which I had never been on before.

The Connector Trail, is a 6.7 mile long trail that connects all the low parts of the three gorges, starting below Stone Door to the west, and climbing up to Hobbs Cabin in the east. It is considered the hardest trail in the park because it winds up and down the rocky slopes of rock fall on the floor of the gulfs. We joined it near Sawmill Campsite, with 3.1 miles to go to Hobbs Cabin. The trail was narrower than any we had been on that day and seemed very lightly traveled. All conversation had pretty much ceased at this point, and we were moving as quick as we could. For 1.4 miles, it went pretty smooth, then we reached the bed of Savage Creek. It was a wide rocky stream bed, covered with fall leaves. There was a little trickle of water running through it that quickly disappeared underground. Looking over the creek bed in the dim afternoon light, I knew that once we entered the woods again, night would soon envelope us. The trail climbed into difficult switchbacks, and our progress slowed dramatically. I started to get cold, but I wasn't going to take the time to dig out another layer. The path was mainly unstable large rocks that were covered in leaves which made for horrible footing. The white blazes were also increasingly hard to find in the dimming light. About halfway up the 1.7 mile climb, we got out our headlamps, and I watched the sun finally sink below the opposing rim. I even tried to take a picture, which really didn't turn out of course.

It was at this point in the trip that I encountered a wonderful feeling that I had not encountered on a hike in a very long time, Mild Concern. Mild Concern is not actual fear for life and limb; that would be called Real Freaking Fear, which I occasionally experience too. Mild Concern is when you are on an outdoor excursion and find that you are faced with the very good possibility for a prolonged period of unpleasantness. This unpleasantness usually takes the form of wandering around in the dark, on the side of a mountain, hungry, slightly dehydrated, legs shaking from exhaustion, and not having any idea when you will reach where you are going. Sure it sounds horrible, but it always makes for good stories. This is the fun stuff!

So we existed in this state of Mild Concern for a while, slipping and sliding our way along, yelling out when we spotted a blaze reflecting in the beam of our headlamps, until the trail took a hard, very steep turn uphill and passed through some large sheer boulders. I knew that we were on the edge of the rim. Things leveled out into a junction of small trails and sign posts, and soon we found the cabin in the still clearing. It was empty. Jack and Rob were happy at the prospect of the inside stay, but I was a little sore about us hauling two tents all day and not using them. This wasn't the first time I carried a tent for no reason, and I got over it quick. It was pitch black night, and we had a complicated meal to cook.

We took over the cabin quick, spreading our stuff out on the bunks and table. There was a very small wood pile beside the porch, but it was not going to be adequate for more than an hour or so. We fanned out into the woods to gather firewood and had a good haul after 30 minutes. I got a good starter fire going in the fireplace, and then I turned my attention to dinner. We had another pasta meal planned. Rob and I got our stoves set up and prepared for our headlamp illuminated culinary adventure. We started boiling water for the pasta and slicing the summer sausage, which we placed in a sierra cup to brown. Then we transferred the cooked sausage to another plate, being careful to keep the grease drippings in the sierra cup. After we got the penne cooking, we added a pesto sauce powder to the grease drippings along with a little pasta water and simmered it to make the sauce. After the pasta finished, we drained it outside and mixed in the sauce and the sausage in a big aluminum pot. There was cooking stuff covering the whole table, and we ended up using every plate, cup, and bowl we had in our mess kits, but it actually worked. It was a really good trail meal. As I sat on the bench at the table and enjoyed it, I was very grateful for the accommodations that we had scored. It would have been very difficult to pull all that off while squatting over logs and rocks.

In warm weather, I will always choose tent camping, but when it is cold, a good shelter is hard to beat. If it is cold, dry weather, tents are still ok, but when you have to sit yourself and your gear in the freezing mud, the idea of a dry place to rest sounds luxurious. Some of my favorite cold weather hiking memories involve shelters. One time in the Smokies we stayed in the shelter on Mt. LeConte in January. The snow was deep, for Tennessee, and the nighttime low got down to 5 degrees. We had carried tents then too, and used the ground cloths to cover the open side of the shelter. We took turns getting firewood from outside and kept the fire going big. I had a thermometer on my jacket zipper. We were keeping it almost 25 degrees inside. I finally fell asleep to the sound of the wind, snapping and beating a loose end of a tarp. It sounded like gun fire. In the morning, the snow reflected the sun so brightly through the openings in our wall that dawn looked like mid-day.

So after the big meal, I slept pretty hard, staying in the top bunk where the warmest air was. The low was around freezing, but it never really got very cold in the cabin. It did get very dark inside once the fire burned down. I got up around 6:30 a.m. and started a small fire back. After the rest of the crew got up, we made breakfast, packed, and drank coffee on the porch while the sun was just coming up over far ridge. After doing a courtesy clean-up of the cabin floor with a scrubby looking broom, we were on the trail by 8:00 a.m. Totally out of water now, we stopped at a small stream on the side of the trail to filter a few liters for the trek out. The North Rim Trail was the same path Jerry and I had taken on our first trip.

It was 8.5 miles back, but I knew it would go fast. We stopped at the first overlook to take pictures, and when we got back on the trail we ran into a group of five backpackers moving very swiftly towards us. It was 9:00 a.m. and between the water stop and the picture stop, we hadn't gone half a mile. Which means, that group had covered 8 miles by 9:00 a.m., meaning that they had probably gotten on the trail a little after 6:00 a.m. Most likely, all of this was so that they could claim the cabin before anyone else. On the remainder of the short trip out, we ran into several more large groups, moving so quickly that you knew they were trying to claim a campsite. I hope some of this has changed with the new reservation system.

The North Rim Trail actually ends at 6.3 miles and the last 2 miles are on the Savage Day Loop, which takes you back to the parking lot. We got back to our cars a little before noon. It was Saturday and the parking lot was completely full. I was very thankful for our little trip in relative solitude, even if it did contain some Mild Concern.

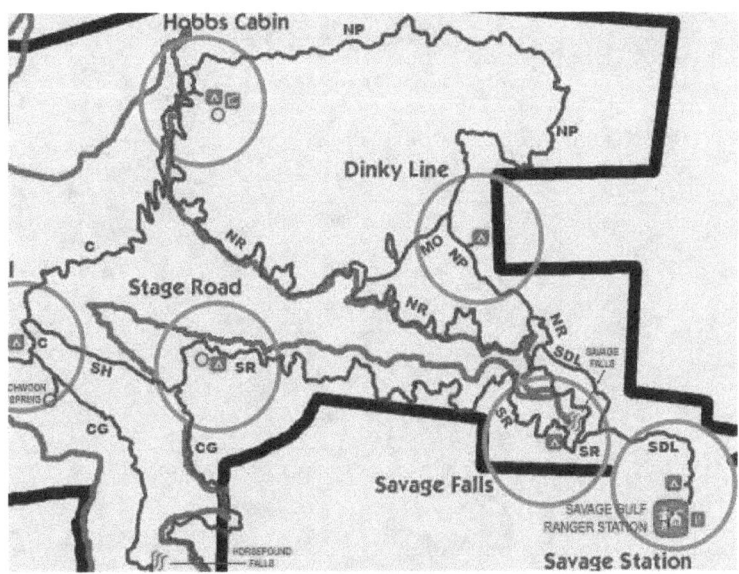

Hobbs Cabin Loop

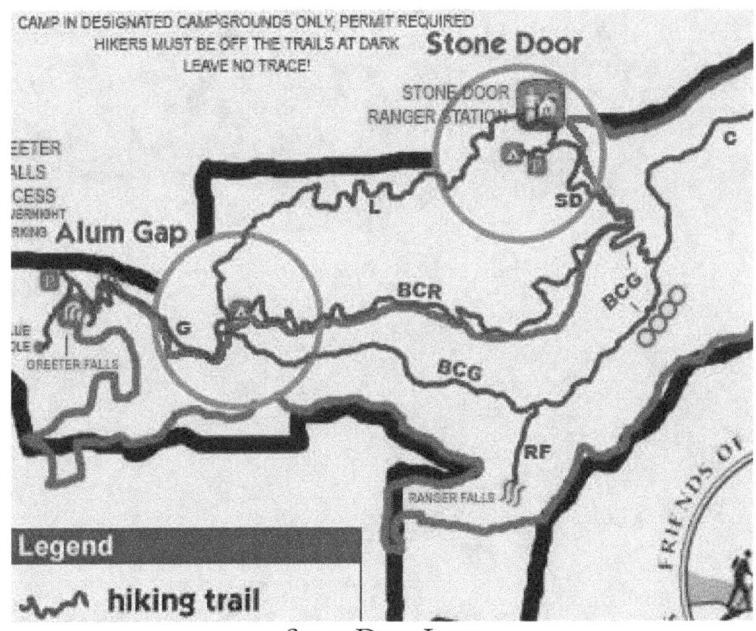

Stone Door Loop

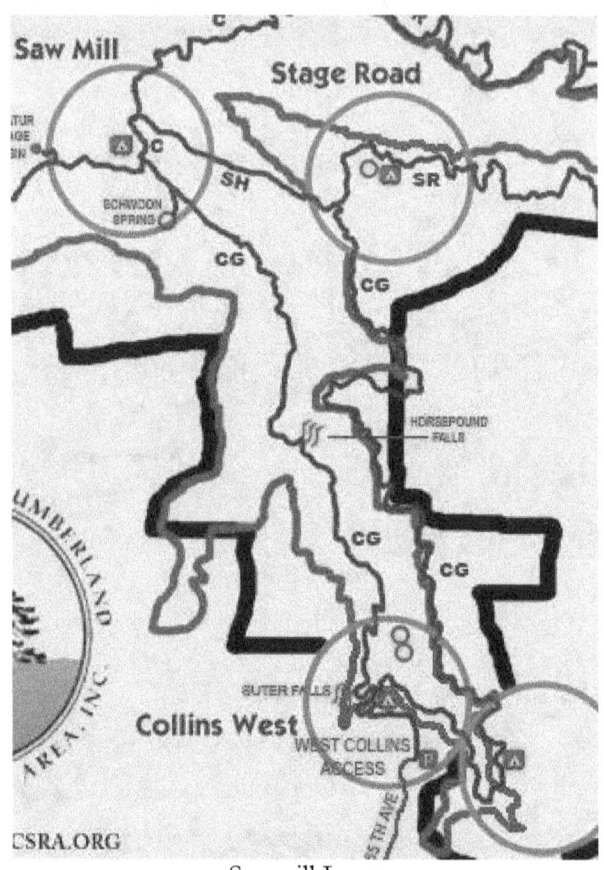

Sawmill Loop

Chapter VII

Fiery Gizzard

Fiery Gizzard is one of larger pieces of South Cumberland State Park and offers the second most overnight backpacking opportunities in the multi-location park after the Savage Gulf and Stone Door area. There are many unusual aspects to this place, but the easiest to notice is the odd name, whose origins are very vague. There is one story of Davey Crockett, who ate a turkey gizzard too quickly from the fire and spit it out into the gorge. Another story is of an Indian chief who threw a turkey gizzard on a fire to make a point during peace talks. In the 1870's, there was an experimental coke furnace built near the gorge that may have been called the same name. The furnace burned for three days and collapsed. In truth, nobody is ever going to know, but it still sounds cool so I hope it always sticks.

I am going to refer to Fiery Gizzard as a park but technically/legally this park is made up of the 233 acre Grundy Forest State Natural Area, the 500 acre Little Gizzard Creek Small Wild Area, the 178 acre Foster Falls Small Wild Area, South Cumberland State Park land, and a lot of private land. And it is that last piece that makes this park a hotbed of controversy. So much so, that the 2014 hike that I am going to describe cannot be legally accomplished today. I will try to explain the story of what is happening using the most current information available, but anyone headed on a trip there should take the time to get an update on the status of the trails. Hiking trails are mostly pretty static things, but in this area they are moving targets.

Fiery Gizzard is a very narrow place, stretching south from edge of Tracy City, across the Grundy County/Marion County line, and ending at the Foster Falls Small Wild Area. The main trail, Fiery Gizzard Trail, stretches the length of the park from north to south, a distance of 12.5 miles. Coming from the north, it weaves its way through the Fiery Gizzard Creek Gorge for about 4 miles, then climbs to the Raven Point overlook, then proceeds along the Plateau to Laurel Gorge, then on to Foster Falls. The only road access is at the Grundy Forest Natural Area parking lot in the north and the Foster Falls parking lot on the southern terminus. The numerous amount of waterfalls, overlooks, and rock formations along its most rugged parts have earned it national recognition as one of the top 25 trails in the U.S. by Backpacker magazine. Unfortunately its fame did not change the legal ownership of some of its most iconic scenery. When the parks were established and the trail was built, much of the private land the trail touched was owned by the Werner Lumber Company. Over the years the descendants were fine doing handshake deals with the State in order to allow the trail to cross their land. Fast forward several decades, these tracts are now owned by much more removed descendants of these families. The owners now live out of state and have no connection whatsoever to land they own, which just happens to contain half of the Fiery Gizzard Trail. This has been a problem that has been recognized for a while and has been on the radar of conservation groups.

We are long past the days of park building through large government funded purchases. When parks get built now, it is primarily through the action of private non-profit groups. One the foremost conservation groups in Tennessee is The Land Trust for Tennessee. Since its founding in 1999, The Land Trust has conserved nearly 100,000 acres of land in Tennessee, 44,000 of which were on the Cumberland Plateau. In 2010, The Land Trust and The Conservation Fund protected 6,100 acres near the Fiery Gizzard trail, ultimately transferring 2,900 acres to the State. In the end this project cost $8 million dollars. To put this in perspective, in 1934, the entire Great Smoky Mountains National Park only cost $12 million.

In 2013, the State received a grant from the U.S. Forest Service Forest Legacy Program, to purchase a working forest conservation easement on 3,282 acres adjacent to the trail area. The conservation easement is a very popular modern tool for land protection. The land stays in private ownership, so it can be sold or passed down through inheritance. However there are restrictions against development in perpetuity. Most of the easements with timber companies allow some type of timber management to continue as well. That probably makes some folks a little disappointed, but at least they won't be blasting a gated community into the side of the gorge.

In late 2014, the legal owner of the Raven Point Campsite, a veterinarian from South Carolina, asked that the trail be removed from his land. He said he would close access to the trail on December 1, 2015, giving the State one year to figure out a re-route. The Raven Point Campsite would be closed permanently. This was the inevitable moment that had been feared and fretted over for the last couple of decades. The owner offered to sell the tract to Friends of South Cumberland for $550,000, then later increased the price to $650,000. He believed that the access to Anderson Falls made the land worth it. Friends of South Cumberland (FSC) got an independent appraisal that listed a value of $265,000. There would be no deal this time. The position of FSC is the same as all other non-profit land conservation organizations. Simply, if you start paying double or triple appraised values for land, then every landowner expects the same, and you will eventually price yourself out of any more acquisitions.

So then the great re-route began, essentially pushing 1.5 miles of trail off the rolling terrain of the Plateau and back into the gorge. Starting in August of 2015, hundreds of volunteers heeded the call and flocked to the edge of the gorge to start blazing trail. In the end the deadline for moving the trail got pushed to December 1, 2016. After this whole affair was publicized, the owner of the 100 acre tract adjacent to the veterinarian, who is a cardiologist in Florida, began to say he also wanted the trail off his land. This was going to add an additional mile to the re-route, however the volunteers and the equipment were already at work and readily accepted the challenge.

Trail building here was not just scraping the leaves and sticks off the ground. The volunteers had to move rocks to build a staircase down 500 vertical feet, then build two bridges, then build another staircase to ascend 500 feet back to the rim. As of March of 2017, the new route was completed. There is still work to be done however, because an entirely new area of the park called Denny Cove was recently acquired, and new trails are currently being constructed.

When I planned my trip, there were four backcountry campsites along the trail. One in the far north near the Day Loop, one near the Raven Point overlook about 4 miles south, one on eastern side of Laurel Gorge, and one near Foster Falls. The Laurel Gorge (Small Wild Campsite) and the Raven Point Campsite were the only true backcountry sites, the other two were less than a half a mile from a parking lot. My plan was to follow Fiery Gizzard trail until the split with Dog Hole Trail, and then follow Dog Hole to Raven Point Campsite. There we would leave our packs and join the Fiery Gizzard Trail as far south as we had safe daylight, hopefully reaching the edge of Laurel Gorge, before returning to our camp. In the morning, we would descend Fiery Gizzard into the gorge and follow it back north to the trailhead. It was really only about 9 miles of actual backpacking, but it was there was no real other option for a loop in a park that is that narrow. Of course, as I pointed out above, the Raven Point Campsite is closed now. The hike I am describing could be easily accomplished as a day hike. If you are looking for a good overnight loop though, it is going to have to come from the south and incorporate the Small Wild Campsite.

It was the last weekend of March when Rob and I met up at a Monteagle gas station off I-24. For me, it had been pouring rain the entire three hour long trip down the interstate. It was 9:00 a.m., but it still almost appeared night. If you read in my Savage Gulf and Stone Door chapter, I commented how hot and dry the weather had always been on those March trips to Savage Gulf. Well, this particular March trip could not have been further removed from that trend. The temperature when we started was in the mid 40's, and it did not stop raining completely until 9:00 p.m. that night.

After grabbing some breakfast, we headed out on to Tracy Road or Highway 41, going east, toward Tracy City. It is important to note that on this route you will pass the headquarters for all of South Cumberland State Park. This is not connected to Fiery Gizzard at all, just keep going. At the very edge of Tracy City, we made a right onto 3rd Street, drove past Tracy Elementary School, took a right on to Marion Street, and then a right on to Fiery Gizzard Road. The road turned gravel at some point, but it felt like we were going to city park instead of a wilderness area. There were a few cars in the parking lot, but we saw no one milling around.

The rain had slowed to a light sprinkle now, but it was still cold and the sky was heavy and dark. Theoretically, the rain was supposed to be moving out, but I would believe it when I saw it. I filled out a damp backcountry permit, writing slowly to not tear it, and put our copy in the plastic bag with my wallet and phone so it would hopefully stay intact. We got our packs on and headed down the Fiery Gizzard Trail/Grundy Forest Day Loop trailhead. The trail began to follow Fiery Gizzard Creek, which was a good sized, whitewater stream that was making a lot of wonderful noise with the flow from the hard rain that had passed through the night before. The miles of trail that follow good mountain streams always seem to go by quicker somehow. There is always something to look at or listen to. We were on the cusp of Spring, but you couldn't tell it from looking in the forest. The woods were brown, gray, and bare. The rain was such that you really couldn't tell how much was falling from the sky and how much was dripping off the trees. We had on our rain jackets at first but took them off, keeping them at easy access in the tops of our packs. At some point at the beginning of our hike Rob realized that he had left his fleece jacket at home on his bed. He had a long sleeve tech shirt and of course his rain jacket, but nothing with very much insulation. We both knew this could be a problem in camp, but had already started hiking. Given the lack of outdoor gear retail outlets in our immediate vicinity, there was nothing we could really do about it.

Heading mostly due south, we passed Blue Hole Falls at 0.5 miles in, then passed the turn off for the Grundy Forest Day Loop at 0.7 miles. Continuing along the Fiery Gizzard Trail, Little Creek and Fiery Gizzard Creeks merge in a cascade at Black Canyon. At 1.3 miles there is a spur trail to Sycamore Falls. Because of the rain, we decided to catch it on the way back the next day. At 1.5 miles the Dog Hole Trail veers to the left and climbs along the bottom of a sandstone bluff, next to a dog hole coal mine. Dog Holes were very small mines that were worked with only a few miners. Often these mines were unlicensed and were mined by people who had no legal right to the coal. I guess it goes along with my reluctance to venture into caves, but you could not pay me to stick my head in a hole like that, much less crawl around and dig.

Soon the Dog Hole Trail to ascends to the eastern rim of the Fiery Gizzard gorge and is intersected by gas pipelines. We were really still at the head of the gorge, and the climb was less than 300 feet. Once we were on top the hiking was easy and fast. About a mile after the gas pipes there is a spur to Yellow Pine Cascades, but we missed it with our quick pace. I was worried about getting a decent site at Raven Point, even though we had not seen any other hikers all day. We did take the spur to Werner Point Overlook at mile 1.9. It was our first real view of the Fiery Gizzard Gorge. The rain finally stopped enough for me to take some pictures. The gorge was around 500 feet deep, not quite as deep as some of the parts of Savage Gulf, but it was significantly narrower. The sides were steep and jagged, with exposed boulder fields under the rim bluffs. Also different from

Savage Gulf, there was an occasional house perched on the opposite ridge, a testament to the precarious ownership status of the park. The wind had picked up and was swirling clouds along the tops of the trees. If it had been the peak of fall foliage season, I would have stayed there for an hour. But there would have been a dozen other folks up there too. In any event, I was glad to get a good overlook out of the wet morning. We pressed on, passing another good overlook, then wound deeper in the woods, away from the rim. At mile 2.8, there was a sign leading to Raven Point Campsite, to the left of the main trail. My worry about a crowded site had been unfounded. We were the only ones there.

We found a good campsite with some decent sitting logs on the exterior of the area. These perimeter spots are always better for both privacy and firewood collection. The woods were open and flat in all directions. It was a little after noon now, and we ate some lunch and packed our daypacks for the remainder of the day. Because nobody was around, we decided that it wasn't worth the time to put our tent up to claim the spot better. If it was a crowded campsite on a nice day, I probably would have wanted to do something a little more permanent than just hang our packs from a tree. Given the continued spitting rain and the lack of human contact, I thought we were pretty safe with our gear hanging from the thick trunk of a hickory. Of course we drew our pack covers down tight, hoping that it didn't come a total monsoon.

We passed the 0.5 mile spur to the Raven Point overlook, thinking we would get back to it either in the afternoon or in the morning. Another half mile later brought us to the spur trail for Anderson Falls. The landscape now was clearly one of private land. I didn't know it at the time, but the property we were walking on is now the subject of the current controversy. There were clear cut areas, old fields, and ATV trails. The spur trail led down a steep, rocky slope and soon joined an elevated wooden staircase that led down another 250 feet to a plunge pool below the 80 foot tall waterfall. The staircase was incredibly rickety, with a single wobbly hand rail. The steps were ice slick from the wet mold and moss growing on them. Every step had to be landed solidly to keep from slipping off the side. We dubbed it the "staircase of death". At the bottom was a decent sized deck that extended over part of the water below the falls. The deck had some lights and wiring on its corners. I guess this was part or maybe all of the $100,000 in improvements claimed by the South Carolina vet. The whole thing was really silly though and was already showing signs of rot. It is a horrible environment for anything made out of lumber. A trail with a decent set of switchbacks would have made a lot more sense. However; the falls themselves were magnificent and as the Plateau goes, they were larger than most anything outside of Fall Creek Falls. The new, re-routed trail comes in to the same spot via the gorge side, so the days of experiencing the staircase of death are thankfully over.

We carefully ascended the stairs and proceeded south along the trail. The landscape was flat and the trail continued to pull away from the edge of the gorge, which meant that mostly our views were restricted to overgrown clear cuts. The trail eventually turned east, towards Laurel Gap, but around 3:30 p.m., we decided to call it. We had hiked probably around 4 miles past Raven Point, but to go another mile to Laurel Gap, would have meant just another mile for the trip back. And honestly, I wasn't sure what was at Laurel Gap anyway, other than an overlook after a steep descent and climb. The rain had actually stopped now, but the sky was still dark, and I really wanted to have a decent amount of time to get the tent set up in the daylight. We got a good pace going on the way back and entered the Raven Point site around 5:00 p.m. There was one other tent on the far side of the area, so the evening was going to remain as quiet as the day had been.

Shortly after we got back to camp, it start to sprinkle rain again. It was some hard work, but we got a decent fire going after about an hour or so. A lot of people get discouraged about building a fire when it is wet or even slightly raining, but it really isn't that difficult as long as you are persistent. Obviously you can't make one in a pouring rain, but once you build up some good heat, you will be surprised how well a fire can withstand precipitation. The best trick I have found throughout the years is to use your knife to whittle the bark off the first several batches of kindling. Then, once you get a small fire going, set the next batch of wood on the perimeter to dry in the heat. Get it close enough to the fire to make it steam, but not burn. If you keep up this rotation as the fire gets bigger, the wood you are adding is getting drier and drier. Of course you can always argue that campfire building is typically a waste of time. But my response is always, "What else you gonna do?"

Now, in this particular case, fire building was kind of an actual necessity, due to Rob's woefully inadequate clothing position. Once we got the fire going enough that we weren't running in all directions to scare up fuel, he really missed his jacket. The low that night was going to be in the mid 30's. The rain had slacked off enough at this point that I let him have my rain jacket and I broke out my down jacket. The extra layer of Gore-Tex wasn't much, but it was better than nothing, and the fire was beginning to decently throw off some heat now. If we had not had the fire, he would just have had to stay in his sleeping bag.

It was dark now, and we still had not eaten. My dinner was a "baked ziti" concoction, consisting of easy-mac, pepperonis, shredded cheddar cheese, parmesan cheese, and crushed red pepper. It was definitely in the top three most disgusting meals that I have ever attempted while backpacking, topping even the summer sausage and tortilla hotdog invention. I was really disappointed because I had made the same thing as a test meal in my kitchen at home, and it was really good. But I have learned too often that until you sit on a cold, wet log over a camp stove and try to cook it, your kitchen trials don't mean much. I even tried to act like it wasn't that bad, but after about four bites I had to dump the rest out. Despite my close held belief that easy-mac holds the possibility for a tasty back country entree, I have never been able to make it work, outside of just making plain easy-mac, which might be the problem. Maybe just plain easy-mac is all it will ever be?

Around 9:00 p.m. the rain completely stopped, and the north wind picked up strong, howling through the bare trees. The temperature began to drop, and I hoped that all of this meant a strong high pressure was pushing all the crappy weather out for good. We eventually left our hard fought campfire, trying to bank it the best we could for the morning.

The dawn broke cold and clear. The skies were quickly turning blue as the welcomed sun began to rise through the trees. You could tell that once the sun came up a little more it was going to be a glorious, early spring day, with bright sunshine and a cool breeze. A handful more days like this would erupt the forest back into the green world of the living. At the end of winter I can never quite remember how things looked with leaves, and I was looking forward to learning it again.

Our banking efforts on the fire had ultimately failed, and there were not enough coals left to get anything going again. We ate a cold breakfast and broke camp quickly, rejoining the trail at around 8:00 a.m. We had not used that much water the day before, and we decided that there was enough remaining for the 4.5 mile hike out. We passed the spur trail to Raven

Point and kept going, ultimately deciding that it wasn't worth the additional mile. After we got back and I read more trail reviews, I really regretted not going to see it. The point is actually a kind of peninsula that extends south off the rim, overlooking the deepest part of the gorge with wide, panoramic views. It is actually on private land, although I have not read anything recently about concerns over losing public access.

As we approached where the Fiery Gizzard Trail dropped off the edge of the gorge, we joked about the wording on the official park map trail description. On the Fiery Gizzard Trail description it read, "The section which starts at the Grundy Forest Natural Area Picnic Shelter and climbs the plateau to Raven Point is possibly one of the most rugged and difficult trails in Tennessee." "Really?", we sarcastically remarked. Those were some pretty bold words to describe a trail that really had less than 1,000 feet of gross elevation change and was on the Cumberland Plateau. I expected it to be just like every other hike out on every other gorge trail I had been on. There would be a steep drop down to the creek, then the trail would gently wind along the drainage, climbing slightly until we reached the Dog Hole Trail junction, and then it would have to climb a little more to get back to the parking lot. I expected us to take not much more than two hours to cover the distance, maybe longer if we decided to take some pictures of the rock formations and the creek. As we moved down the slick, muddy switchbacks, I openly lectured, to my audience of one, how you have to take any trail descriptions for the eastern U.S. with a grain of salt and how the population is so sedentary and out of shape that anything other than a paved sidewalk is called moderately strenuous. The switchbacks seemed to end early, far above the creek, and then the trail abruptly ended in a towering boulder field. My lecture series was over.

The boulder field was nearly 200 yards long and was pretty much crossed by jumping only. I was relieved when we reached the end, and the trail began to descend toward the water, which I could hear now. "This is more like it!", I thought. We barely traveled 50 yards on the trail. I was just catching a glimpse of the whitewater through the trees, when the trail ended again. In front of us was a jumble of rocks that ascended a good 50 vertical feet. We crawled our way to the top to find another 100 yard long boulder field. After rock hopping this one, the trail descended again. It leveled out for a few dozen yards, and then climbed rocks for nearly 100 feet in elevation. At the top was another boulder field. "What in the hell?", was

77

our collective response. I began to look harder at the terrain and thought about what I had seen on the overlooks the day before. It appeared to me that as erosion wore away at the narrow, steep sides of the gorge, a large number of rock slides had occurred. These rock slides left large swaths of boulders strewn along the already steep angle of the gorge wall, leading all the way to the creek below. The Fiery Gizzard Trail, had no other route than to climb over and through these mazes of stone.

Well, we were in it, and there was only one thing to do and that was press on through. The coolness of the morning was quickly gone. We were sweating now with our sleeves rolled up. It would have been a hard day hiking trail without the 40 pound packs, but with the extra load it really was some of the hardest terrain I have ever backpacked through. After a while we even quit cussing. It wasn't worth the breath. For 2.5 miles, we clawed, crawled, jumped, and slid our way through this seemingly endless boulder field nightmare. We kept a strong pace, mainly because we were so annoyed that we were trying to get to a more enjoyable stretch of trail as soon as possible. It never materialized, we just had to keep going. We passed over the house size boulders of the Fruit Bowl and barely even noticed them. Then, out of nowhere, hiking trail actually became a hiking trail again, right near where the Dog Hole Trail junction was. I have never been more relieved just to see a stretch of dirt that lasted for more than 100 yards.

Then of course came the crowds. It was a beautiful Sunday morning after all, and I bet we encountered more than 50 people coming down from the Grundy Forest parking area. They all looked so clean and energetic. I had a strong urge to warn them about how hard it was. Of course I didn't. They were safely exploring, and I would never rob anyone of that with discouragement, no matter how well meaning it was. I have encountered many people on trails that have told me that it was too hard up ahead and that I should turn around immediately. I have never followed their advice, and I have never regretted it.

We took a slight detour to Sycamore Falls. This was really the first time we stopped all morning. The last half mile before the parking lot seemed to be about as busy as a city sidewalk. We got back to the parking lot a little after 11:00 a.m. In the end it took us well over 3 hours to cover 4.5 miles of trail, and we literally only stopped once. The meager granola bars for breakfast had run out a long time before, and I was still kind of hungry from my failed dinner. We were ready for our victory meal.

A victory meal is any meal that you eat after surviving a hard day or days of physical exertion. It is the grown up version of the little league season ending pizza party. Typically speaking, the more exhausted you are, and the longer without decent food to eat, the better the victory meal is. My first ever backpacking victory meal was at a Shoney's in Maryville, TN. It was the third day of a Smokies backpacking trip from Fontana Dam to Cades Cove, in December. We had hiked in the dark, with one flashlight, for over six miles, just to reach a vehicle. Of course it was freezing cold and misting rain. We drove for nearly an hour to reach civilization and checked into a Red Roof Inn. Shoney's was in walking distance and was pretty much the only restaurant open. I had the Shoney's version of surf and turf. Still today it is one of the best meals I have ever eaten.

This particular victory meal was at the Waffle House in Monteagle. It was a good meal, but the most entertaining part of the meal was getting to sit in a booth behind a group of University of the South (also referred to as Sewanee) students. Of course, in a way, they were the typical group of college students eating out at mid-day on Sunday. They had just woken up and were still in recovery mode from Saturday night. But their conversation was unlike anything I was ever around when I was 20 years old and attending UT Martin. They were discussing their summer plans. One was going to an internship in New York, with the United Nations. One was going to an internship in Washington D.C. One was attending an art school in Berkley. One was going to work at the U.S. embassy, in Warsaw, Poland. And of course, they were all complaining about it.

So after finishing our brunch with the 1 percenter kids, we said our goodbyes and hit the road. If there was a theme to this trip, I would have to say it was "You are never too experienced to make mistakes." It would be easy to list the mistakes made, such as Rob forgetting his jacket, my disastrous attempt at easy-mac baked ziti, willfully skipping the main overlook in the whole park, and arrogantly discounting the warnings from the guide about the difficulty of the trail. But the biggest mistake that was made was one that I didn't begin to realize until after I got home. When we got off the trail, I felt completely fine. I had run a half marathon the weekend before, so I really had none of the stiffness and soreness that are typical when you end a couple of days of backpacking. Of course I had excuses, but I didn't train properly for the race, and ended up trying to cram all of my long runs in during the three weeks leading up to the event. After the race, I noticed a little soreness in my left foot, but I ignored it, thinking it was just part of the normal post-race stiffness. When we set out on our hike, I felt it a little first, then it went away. I thought nothing of it. On the second day, when we were jumping from boulder to boulder for miles, I typically led off with my left foot (I am left handed). Of course I had an extra 40 pounds on my back, and I was wearing my Asolo backpacking boots, which are really light mountaineering boots and have little cushion in the soles. Anyway, when I stepped out of the car after the 3 hour drive back, I felt a sharp pain in my foot. It stayed with me the rest of the evening, and when I got up the next morning it was just as intense with each step. By that afternoon I could barely put any weight on my foot at all. It ended up being a stress fracture, which took a couple of months to recover from. It was an annoying mistake, but if I had repeated it on a big mountain trip in the Rockies or Cascades, it could have turned out worse.

So from this little two day adventure I walked/hobbled away with a bunch of important lessons; remember your jacket in winter, believe the trail guide and follow it, don't run a half marathon and jump up and down on sandstone for 2.5 miles in the same week, and sometimes easy-mac is just left better as easy-mac.

This map represents the most recent developments. Some of the route we took on the northern half of the hike is no longer on the rim, but has been routed back into the gorge.

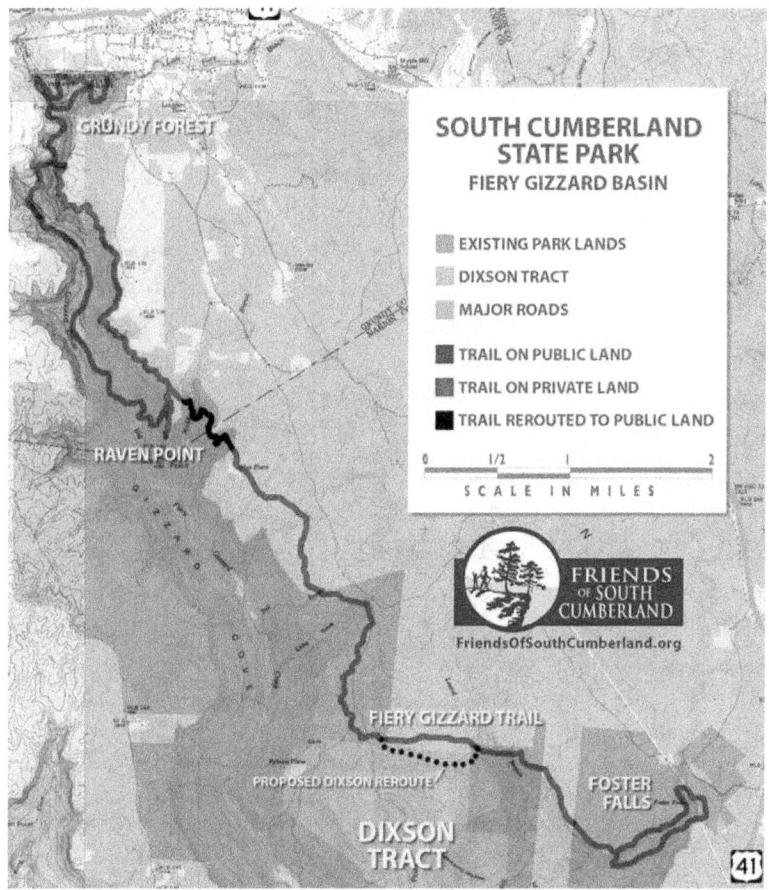

Chapter VIII

Cumberland Trail – Tennessee Gorge

The State of Tennessee is blessed with a lot of waterways, but the most culturally iconic, is the 652 mile long Tennessee River. Although the great Mississippi River forms the western border of Tennessee, it is the Tennessee River that has had the largest role in the State's historical settlement, military history, industrial development, and tourism industry. Without the Tennessee River, our state wouldn't have had the Battle of Shiloh, our role in the Manhattan Project, or a place to throw the goal post after beating the Florida Gators. Of course, it isn't totally just a Tennessee river, it cuts across the entirety of northern Alabama, forms a little piece of the state line with Mississippi, and crosses the narrow western tip of Kentucky, where it empties into the Ohio River. As I mentioned in the introduction, the Tennessee was a highway for the settlers as they moved west. In many places it had a swift moving, rapid filled current, that was treacherous to travel, but much faster than trying drive a wagon over the Cumberland Plateau and Highland Rim. Today, the raging river that the flotillas of flat bottom boats valiantly braved, has been buried under a continuous series of lakes managed by the Tennessee Valley Authority. The "river" is still culturally important as a place of recreation and industry, but there is not much actual river remaining.

The majority of the Tennessee is contained in a very wide valley, with hilly bluffs that define the immediate shores, followed by gently sloping land that forms far off ridges. These valleys have all been flooded, some to a greater degree than others. Between the headwaters near Knoxville, and the junction with the Ohio at Paducah, KY, the river loses about 500 feet in elevation, which leaves a lot of room for dams or impoundments of various heights. However; in the midst of all of the locks, river marinas, power plants, and housing developments, there is a little 27 mile section of the river near Chattanooga that kind of resembles what Hernando De Soto saw in 1540, or what the Native Americans saw for 7,500 years before that.

The Tennessee Gorge, is a winding piece of the Tennessee River that squeezes through a narrow gap, connecting the Tennessee Valley in the east to the Sequatchie Valley in the west. It is 1,000 feet deep, with steep, sharp slopes extending from the water's edge, up to sheer bluffs which line the gorge's rim. Historically, this was one of the most dangerous stretches of the river for travelers, with named rapids such as The Pot, The Pan, The Skillet, and The Suck. In 1913, the Hales Bar Dam, today the site of Nickajack Dam, flooded the rapids, but the narrow, swift current still flows the same course, just with deeper water.

One look at the gorge, and you know it is a special place. During the 1970's the hills and ridges surrounding Chattanooga began to sprout more and more housing developments. In 1981, a few Chattanooga residents created The Tennessee River Gorge Trust with the goal of protecting the land encompassed by the gorge. Today, of the 27,000 acres in the gorge area, 17,000 acres have been placed under some form of protection, some of it under direct ownership of the Trust. While the most of the Cumberland Plateau has been spared major development due to the lack of close population centers, the area near Chattanooga was the most vulnerable to the developer's bulldozer. If it had not been for the efforts of a few concerned individuals, it is very conceivable that today the Tennessee Gorge would be a subdivision address and not a hiking location.

To be completely honest, I didn't read or research much about the Tennessee Gorge in my initial planning for this November backpacking trip. I was wanting to hike a section of the Cumberland Trail for the first time, and I was looking for the shortest travel distance. During my research I found that the trail system of the Cumberland Trail near Chattanooga also contained the option for a loop hike, as opposed to the normal point to point layout on the other sections. The loop hike, along with the easy and quick access off I-24, easily sold me on the Tennessee Gorge section.

It was just going to be an overnight trip, Saturday morning to Sunday afternoon. The skies that Friday had been lead gray, and there was a warmness to the air with a few scraps of early fall humidity. There was no doubt that rain was coming. It was coming to bash down the remnants of the last bright leaves and to settle down all the flying seed life of the autumn. When the rain finally started after sunset, the drops came in slow. The slow rains had just started to come about a month before, and it was an adjustment to think about weather in terms of days rather than hours.

At one time, we had upwards of six people committed, but a series of scheduling conflicts, sicknesses, and family emergencies, had dwindled the number down to just two, Rob and myself. Of course, trips only go in two directions, they either balloon in number of participants or shrink. I have always thought that a four person trip is the best number, enough people to have a good conversation and get camp work done, but not so many that it slows down moving or makes it hard to find a campsite. However; it is usually difficult to really plan for a certain number. The best practice is to just invite everyone and see how it shakes out. And in reality, it wasn't going to really be a two man trip. Rob was going to bring his Jack Russell Terrier, Molly, along with us. Hiking with a dog was completely uncharted territory for me.

For some reason on this trip I had all of these crazy ideas about going ultralight. I would carry just a fleece sleeping bag, a light tarp to make a bivy sack, and leave my stove. Then the first few frosty nights hit in November, and all of a sudden I remembered what real cold felt like, something I had forgotten since April. I backed off my Survivor Man plan for the most part but kept a few of my ideas. I decided to carry only one extra pair of socks, about four less than I normally do. My food consisted of two bags of Chex mix, a bag of peanut M&Ms, four small granola bars, a 6 oz summer sausage, and two flour tortillas, all neatly packed into a single freezer bag. I was also able to get all of my clothes into a single freezer bag as well. This trip was also going to be a test for my newly acquired tent, which I had bought that Friday afternoon. I took it straight out of the box and packed it in my bag. I hoped they included everything on the assembly line.

Around 5:00 a.m. I headed outside into the dark, windy drizzle. The drizzle turned into a full sprinkle by the time I got onto the interstate heading west, and soon the full sprinkle turned into a steady rain that wanted to push my car into the median. Finally a faint, smothered dawn emerged. I knew it was probably about the brightest it would be for most of the day.

As I drove up the Plateau and began the descent down to Chattanooga, I looked to the north. There were light wisps of white clouds swirling along the ragged bluffs that top the pile of ridges on the left hand side of the road. I had stared into this country at least a dozen times over the past few years, but each time saw me on a tight schedule going to or from some place incredibly important. But today was different. Today I was going to go see what was there.

Getting to this area is not very difficult, but finding the trailhead is a little dicey. Just take I-24 to exit 178 (on the western side of Chattanooga) and then take US 27 going north. At the US 27 and US 127 junction, take 127 for 1.6 miles and turn left onto TN 27, which climbs the Plateau. After 8.1 miles you will turn left to enter Prentice Cooper State Forest, and the trailhead is 3.2 miles down Tower Drive. We were on the right path the whole time but after the roads turn to gravel they also quit being marked, so we ended up flagging down a passing vehicle to ask for directions. There are some more detailed directions at cumberlandtrail.org which I would check out before planning a trip. The trailhead area is actually pretty nice. There was probably room for twenty cars, and the site was additionally equipped with a vault toilet, a large covered map which housed a trail log, and a few garbage cans. I actually felt confident our cars would still be there when we returned the next day. I had thought we would have been lucky to get a wide spot in the road and a metal fence post with a piece of reflective tape as a trail head marker.

It was 10:45 a.m., and this was the first time I had been outside for more than thirty seconds all morning. Instantly I was met with the gray bite of a winter's day in the air. Even with my fleece I was cold near the point of shivering, but I knew I would warm up soon enough. We set to work getting ready. Rob brought out Molly, who quickly began working out her energy by streaking about the parking lot. There was not too much to assemble. I gave Rob the tent poles and the fuel canister for the stove, we laced up our boots, and were trail bound within five minutes of getting out the car, underlining again how much faster everything is with two people. I swear I have been on some large group trips were it takes us an hour to get from the parking lot into the woods. We walked over to the map and the log to write our information down, arbitrarily planning our trip as we stood there.

We decided upon first going north along the long side of the Mullin's Cove Loop trail, which would take us eventually south to the Hemlock Branch campsite on the southern terminus of the loop. Depending on when we got there we would decide whether to camp, or head down the Pot Point Loop trail, which was further south. Either way, by going north first and doing the long side of the loop, we were trying to assure that the hike out on Sunday would be a shorter day. It would be just a straight shot north from Snoopers Rock Overlook, along the rim of the main gorge, and through Indian Rockhouse and Stone Door. Considering just the main loop, it was 9.8 miles in all.

Now we were assured of where we were going, we actually had to start. We walked across the road to view a trail sign that pointed nowhere near where we wanted. We crossed the road back to the parking lot where this time we did see a faint start of a trail off to the left, back corner of the parking lot. We now were on our way, shuffling through the heavy wet leaves, Molly staying close and weaving in and out of our long, early strides.

The trail was almost level through the new growth forest, and I was thinking we would make a good three miles an hour. The forest here was new growth enough where there was little underbrush, but all the tree trunks were small in diameter. Because of the thick red and yellow carpet of maple and hickory leaves, the trail was only visible as a wider swath where there were no fallen limbs, green briars, or saplings. It was not raining now, but the soaked landscape had about the same effect. The constant droplets of water fell off every heavy leaf from fifty feet above us. Of course the water from the trail seemed to soak the bottom half of our pants through some mysterious osmosis.

My time projections changed quick when we started down a series of slick boulders along the steep side of a gorge. If there was any friction remaining between the soles of our shoes and the wet surface of the rock, it was easily defeated by the layers of wet leaves which were slickly plastered over the trail. The hike had now turned into more of a slide and most often our progress was only checked by shins and ankles sliding into another rock or by grabbing onto saplings and overhanging branches to steady ourselves. At first the slope seemed slight but soon we found ourselves going down terrain that would have been a meticulous rock hop in dry conditions. It felt like we were skating as we wound up and down the stair step like boulders which lined the creek bed at the bottom of the gorge. The going was painstaking, the path was sometimes hard to find, but overall it was fun, much more so than the quick strides we had on the flat ground above us. I lowered my ground coverage estimation for the day happily. Other than stopping once to take off my fleece, we kept as quick as pace as possible. Although Molly was not on a leash, she never moved more than ten feet away from Rob, and managed to bound over the ragged boulders that stood four times her height like they were couches in her living room.

After about thirty or forty-five minutes of hard going, we reached a steep slope off to our left. Although we had followed a shallow creek the entire time, we never crossed it and it looked like now it was time to regain the high ground. I was slightly relieved. Although the slick boulder skating had been entertaining, I knew that four more hours of it was going to amount to a very long day. The fern strewn slope seemed to end about fifty feet above us, and the trail followed it straight up.

On the climb we ran into the only other hikers we would encounter that day. Once on top of the bluff, the country started to flatten out a little more like it was when we started. I knew we would be fine in making the campsite and would probably have some additional time for a short excursion beyond. I could not see much of the parallel side of the gorge but I could tell it was deepening. The wind was picking up and the leaves were even thicker now. It was getting hard to hear parts of our meandering conversation.

From nowhere it started to rain hard, and we frantically threw off our packs and dug out our rain jackets and pack covers. Just as we finally got settled and hiking again, of course the rain stopped. As soon as I would think how silly it was for us to have stopped and put on all the rain gear, the drops would come again. I would pull the hood of my jacket back up and be lost in my own world, with a narrow view forward, protected from the outside, with the drum beat of the drops on the leaves drowning out all sound but my own thoughts. I have always liked to walk in the rain. When I was in college, I would always take the long way to class through the quad on rainy days.

The rain slacked up and eventually stopped. After crossing a jeep trail, we crossed a creek by a sign which read 2.2 miles to Mullins Cove Overlook. I was once again surprised at the consistency in trail markers and signs, contrasting this new, completely privately built and maintained trail with the long established trails that we had encountered in the past.

When we finally crossed over on the other side of the ridge, I could tell that there was a much more significant drop off to the west now. I could not see much other than the wall of orange and red that made up the opposing side of this gorge. There was a line of rocky cliffs which peaked beneath the canopy about 30 feet down from the crest, and it kept going west until the other wall of our gorge blocked the view. I didn't need the map to know that we were getting close to Mullins Cove Overlook, which also was our designated lunch stop. This was a very good thing too, because it was getting on past 2:00 p.m., and my 9:00 a.m. McDonalds breakfast was running low.

There was a sign reading "Mullins Cove Overlook" plainly placed in almost the middle of the trail. A narrow spur came into sight, leading steeply down to the right. It went down the slope of the ridge for about 15 yards, and then there was a cluster of large boulders which protruded out over the gorge. The rocks lay stair stepped, and we quickly bounded down to the furthest point on the last one, which was the most level and flat of them all. The creek, about 500 feet below us, was hidden in the burning canvas of color but you could trace the route along the bottom, all the way south until it hit the opposing perpendicular ridge we had been watching. Then it turned to reveal a peep of the Tennessee River at the very end where the gorge opened out wide. The water still seemed to shine despite the gloom. The sky was still gray, but in varying shades, and the darkness of the day only made the late autumn leaves seem that much richer. There were webs of clouds clinging to the battlements of stone cliffs that bounded each surrounding ridge. The view was almost completely open except for a handful of yellow maple branches swaying in the stormy breeze. We took our pictures, and then climbed back up to our packs to retrieve our lunches. I set in a small impression behind the farthest, flattest rock and made a kingly spread out of my water, trail mix, and peanut M&Ms. Rob sat on a boulder off to the right, and Molly begged for food between us. She got several handfuls of each of our lunches. She had more than deserved it. After eating, we took a few more pictures, trying to capture as much as possible. I could have stayed the rest of the day on those cliff tops, but the fall afternoon was burning quick, and I knew we needed to find our campsite soon.

After the overlook, the trail turned east, which was good because that was what it was supposed to do. We had barely been walking for more than ten minutes when we stumbled directly into the Hemlock Branch campsite. Like everything else on the trail, it was done right. Placed in a wide, relatively flat area along side of a shallow creek, there were several spots for tents, a fire ring, and even a stone bench which was augmented by a backrest woven out of small branches. There was even a good pack hanging tree. We were barely able to take it all in, because as soon as we stopped the rain began to pick back up. Eventually, the pace of the drops began to be too much to ignore, and I had to cram everything back into my pack while tearing the tent bag out of the bottom of the now tangled mess of stuff sacks and zip lock bags. While we were spreading out the ground cloth, we got a merciful small break in the rain which allowed us to keep the inside completely dry.

My tent was up in less than five minutes. As we snapped the last rain fly clip, the wind died and the drops ceased falling. I was seriously impressed by both the space inside the tent and the fact that all of the pieces seemed to have been included. The rain continued in spurts and it seemed to be getting colder by the minute. It felt like it could easily start snowing.

I knew that we needed to get going if there was going to be more to our day than the six mile hike in. When the weather is that crappy, great expectations are the only destinations that get you away from your tent. Well that and the complete boredom that sets in with a set up camp and two hours of daylight left. So after a quick consultation of the now excessively creased map in a zip lock bag, we decided to continue down the Pot Point Loop trail, going south until we hit Ransom Hollow Overlook. It looked like about a 1.5 mile hike down to it and without our packs we knew we should be able to make it quickly.

It was 3:15 p.m. when we crossed the creek by our campsite and climbed a steep slope. We were barely out of sight of the camp when we lost the trail for about 10 minutes. In the thick leaves we were sometimes completely dependent on the trail markers. Once we were headed in the right direction, I started to get a little concerned about the fact that neither one of us was carrying a headlamp. Not sure what happened there. In any event, we declared a 4:30 p.m. turnaround time and swore to stick to it.

The leaves seemed to be getting thicker and thicker, and it was apparent that this was a much less traveled route than the northern loop we had been on. We were headed solidly south now, and we could see glimpses of Mullins Creek far down the gentle slope that swept off to our right. Finally around 4:00 p.m. we came to what looked like a trail intersection with some kind of jeep trail. There was a sign that said Ransom Hollow Overlook. We didn't see any sign of a spur trail, and I had thought that we had lost so much elevation that there just could not be much of an overlook anyway. We cussed a little, chocked it up to an unfinished trail, and turned around.

We had passed under some bluffs on our way there, and I was determined to have something to show for the trail, even if it was a little impromptu bouldering. We picked our way through the rocks pretty easy, with Rob lifting Molly to the step above him and then climbing up. The summit boulders were just large slabs of limestone laying at sharp angles and we tried to get every ounce of traction possible on the almost smooth, featureless, wet rock. A few more yards of crawling and we crossed over the crest of one of the slabs and onto an almost even and flat slab at the very top. There was no real view, just the thick tops of the trees staring at the other thick tops of trees, nothing much different than what we were seeing from the trail other than a little more gray sky and water. Disappointing view or not, it was still a picture taking accomplishment.

It was a little after 5:00 p.m. when we got back to camp. My boots had reached their saturation point in the wet conditions, and my socks were finally wet. Rob took Molly, who was shivering, into the tent to dry her off and feed her. I had no problem gathering a big pile of sticks and once Rob had Molly burrowed in his sleeping bag he helped me strip the bark off to get some decent kindling. Everything was still soaking wet but we had a good fire going in about an hour. It was almost as good as dark by now, and it was long past time to eat. We laid out our cooking stuff on the log laying where there was no smoke blowing. I began my experimental meal consisting of a summer sausage and a tortilla. The intent was some sort of hot dog like creation. I cut off half the sausage and skewered it on a sharp stick and stuck it over the best flame we had. In a few minutes it was half blackened and spitting hot juice which flared up in the coals below it. Then I drew the smoldering meat out of the fire and placed it inside one of the tortillas. Rob was just now finishing hydrating his package of stew, and we both sat down on the rock bench to our dinners.

My creation was a disgusting disaster. It tasted like a burned piece of summer sausage wrapped in a cold tortilla. Which is what it was. I chewed it quick, threw the other part of the sausage in the fire, ate the second tortilla, and filled up on trail mix and M&Ms. We piled up a little more firewood and settled into the drifting conversation of the campfire. It was cold, but not so cold where you couldn't keep your hands out of your pockets. Sometimes the wind would pick up and there would seem to be little specs of white falling through the beams of our head lamps. We would think it was raining or snowing, but we could never see anything hitting our clothes. Then a minute later we would look up through the thinning canopy swaying above us and see a few stars and sharp black sky. A minute later there would be nothing again but a gun barrel sky of night clouds. We ran out of dry wood before we ran out of conversation, but it was time to wrap up the day anyway. Molly had not moved since we got back to camp and was asleep still in Rob's sleeping bag. It had been a hard day for such a little dog. Even though I fell asleep quickly, she laid so still with Rob that it never even felt like there was a dog in our tent.

I slept all the way through to the gray dawn. The cold wet boots and the cold wet socks were sitting under the vestibule, and they did not act as much of a motivating force. The boots were as unpleasant as I had imagined but at least they were not frozen. None of my socks that I laid out on a low branch had dried at all. I had changed into my only spare dry pair of socks when we got back from the ill-fated day hike. The ultra-light strategy of carrying less dry socks seemed pretty stupid now. I retrieved our makeshift bear bag, which consisted of lazily putting two freezer bags of food balanced on top of a bent over sapling. You can usually get away with that on the Plateau.

We needed to filter water so I hopped down into the stream bed and found some good footing on a little island of rocks and filled up a liter bottle. By the time I made it back up the bank, Rob was already stirring around with his food. We lit up the stove and warmed some water, first for Molly's food, then for our coffee, a liquid concentrate mix which turned out okay, though I must admit that I still like the cappuccino powder mix that I always carry. The fire ring was nothing but cold ashes. You could not even smell where smoke had been, but we stood around it anyway and ate our breakfast of granola bars. As we packed the tent up it started to snow for a few minutes.

It was 9:45 a.m. by the time we crossed the stream once more, now with full pack. Almost all my food was gone now and with only a liter of water, my pack seemed to weigh nothing. The sun was still buried deep under heavy gray clouds, and the temperature seemed stuck around 40 degrees. In twenty minutes we crossed the same logging road that we had started on, walking past a single parked car. The ground was flat now with thick undergrowth, and the trail was muddy. Soon a rocky bluff appeared to loom over the left side of the trail, and then the whole front of the forest opened up into the sky and the horizon as we stepped onto Snooper's Overlook.

Snooper's Overlook is a 200 square foot, flat boulder that juts out from a cliff line of the gorge in a sharp bend of the Tennessee River. There were barely perceivable ripples in the water more than 500 feet below us, and I could see them move in the leaf choked eddies along the white boulders lining the shore. There was still no sun in the overcast sky, but more light than the day before. The brighter half of the southern sky made the colors burn different than they had on Mullins Cove. There were two men already there that had very nice cameras set up and were starting to take pictures. Rob and I stood out of their way and struck up a conversation. We told them about our attempt at seeing Ransom Hollow Overlook. They told us that we turned around only with a hundred yards to go down that jeep trial. Oh well, at least we climbed those random rocks.

Of course we got plenty of good pictures, but honestly it was one of those views where all the shots looked professional. You couldn't take a bad picture if you tried. Of all of my fall trips, this is one of the rare ones where the fall foliage pictures actually turned out. The perfect amount of sunlight is really needed to make the picture turn out close to what your eye is perceiving. It was getting on near 10:45 a.m. when we hopped down from the block of stone, and headed back onto the trail which snaked up the bluff we had passed. The two photographers were still staring hard to the horizon and not saying a word to one another.

We kept moving north, with the river staying on our right. Occasionally there would be a small clearing where one could attempt to find some kind of an open lookout if that person had not been already spoiled by Snooper's. The undergrowth was thick again because we were so close to the bluffs. There were frequent blown down trees across the trail, but we kept up our quick pace despite losing the trail for a few minutes on a steep set of switchbacks. We ran into two hunters that were holding a radio receiver and looking for their lost coon dog, a quick reminder that we were hiking in a TWRA Wildlife Management Area, not a State Park.

The trail got mildly steep for the first time all day, and we began to pull out of sight of the river. Stopping to catch our breath, and almost getting hot for the first time, we saw a cluster of rocks ahead marked with a sign. There was an overhanging bluff and then a rocky scramble that led around it. On top of the scramble we came to where the trail passed up and through a two and half foot wide crack in the back of the slab that made up the lower bluff. There were stairs to assist up the 30 foot stretch. I had to take Rob's sleeping pad off his pack for him to fit through. This feature is called Stone Door, and it is a miniature version of the other Stone Door that is adjacent to Savage Gulf.

Once on top we stopped to look around for a few seconds and covered the last half a mile at a getting home pace. We were pretty much on top of everything now. The trail was easy flat all the way back to the road and the parking lot. The cars were covered with the leaves that had thickened on the ground during our night stay. As soon as I took off my pack I realized how cold I was going to be in about two minutes and dug into my trunk for dry clothes and shoes, which I always carry for occasions such as these. Molly was happy to be back too, and Rob didn't have to coax her to get her to jump into the back seat. After that trip she could have looked down on an Iditarod champion Huskie. We sorted our gear back out, loaded up, and said goodbye. I ate my victory meal on the road. As I looked back off to the north at the piles of gray bluffs still being streamed over by the dirty white clouds, I thought about how this time I knew what was up there, and I was glad to know it.

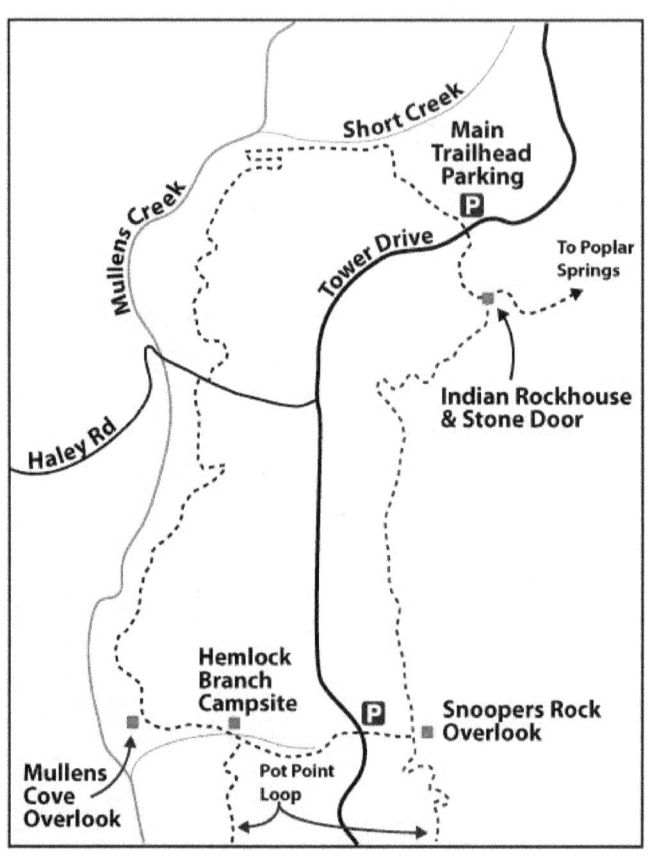

Chapter IX

Elk River Float

After that scouting hike on the Obed Gorge, I had my eyes set on a good canoe excursion. I had a lot of fond memories about the last time I held a canoe paddle in my hand. When I was in college, we went on a three day, 35 mile trip down the Buffalo River in the Arkansas' Ozarks. It was the middle of March, our spring break, and the outfitter launched us into the shallow, rapid filled water while a light snow was falling. There were six of us in three canoes, and it took over an hour to get half a mile down the river because we all turned over at least once, typically by the strong current launching the boat up onto boulder laying low in the water. Every time someone flipped we had to fish our gear out of the river that wasn't tied down, then drag the canoe over to the bank, dump the water out and repack everything, only to go a couple hundred yards and do it all again. Our clothes were almost entirely soaked in the freezing water. The snow continued to fall around us. We were in a deep rocky gorge inside a national forest. There was no easy escape, with only a couple of high bridges spanning the gorge. I wasn't sure how we were going to ever make it to our rendezvous over 30 miles downriver. By the time the sun started to sink low over the ridges above us we found a spot to camp and set up our soaked gear. Temperatures got down in the 20's that night. By morning, nothing dried and now it was covered in ice. We kept searching the map for a possible way to shorten the trip but there was just no way to do it. Somehow by noon the second day we found our groove, quit flipping, and made some real mileage. The last morning we ate a good breakfast with eggs and country ham, and floated the remaining miles, arriving at the rendezvous point that afternoon with a couple of hours to spare. We had brought our fishing gear and bought out of state permits, but the trip had been so rough that we had not spared the time to fish. We took advantage of the first bit of free time we had and gave it a try. The sun had finally come out and a warm spell had started. I stood in the river with my shirt off, glorious warm sun on my back (which can only be appreciated after unceasing cold for a couple of days), and fished, while standing under this 500 foot high cliff and watching the clouds roll by.

Even after all of the big mountain trips I have been on in the years since college, those days on the Buffalo count as one of my favorites.

So when I set out to plan this adventure, I first looked to the Obed area. There are no commercial outfitters on the Obed, but the water and terrain are similar in the Big South Fork National River and Recreation Area. Big South Fork is a park that straddles the Tennessee and Kentucky state line, north of Crossville, near Oneida, TN. It is a park of steep gorges that contains both the Big South Fork and upper Cumberland River. I went on a day canoe trip on the Cumberland River while in college. Of course like almost every other river in the South, it is dammed. The water was high, and we basically paddled a 15 mile stretch of lake. There are several white water sections of the Big South Fork that a guide service rents canoes on, but you basically have to prove that you have adequate Class II paddling experience for them to allow you to take the trip. After several rounds of e-mails they were unable to tell me where I could even get the type of experience that they wanted. After I looked at the five hour drive for us and unsure availability of canoes, I gave up on Big South Fork, thinking surely there had to be another good river for a multi-day trip. I spent hours combing the internet, with one search page going and one Google map open. I looked at the Red River near Clarksville (where you can float by the Bell Witch Cave, another Tennessee cave I will not be going in), the Duck River and Harpeth River in Middle Tennessee, the Flint River in northern Alabama, the Green River in central Kentucky, the Caney Fork River and the Sequatchie River in the central Plateau, and the Hiawassee River in the foothills of the Appalachians. There was a different story for all of them, but either I couldn't find an outfitter that would do a multi-day canoe float, or there was simply not enough free flowing water left to run more than a day without lake paddling.

As much as I love Tennessee and the adjacent wild areas of our border states, this whole region is a graveyard of rivers. It is like somehow for 50 or 75 years, every time someone looked at a natural flowing creek, stream, or river, this irresistible idea came into their consciousness, "Let's like totally destroy that!" I understand the big dams on the big parts of the Cumberland and Tennessee Rivers that make the waterways navigable for barges and make lots of hydroelectricity. But I don't get the dozens of other dams that flood out hundreds of miles of what was beautiful creation in the name of flood control and recreational lakes. I don't understand why every river in West Tennessee other than the Hatchie (Tennessee's other Scenic river under Federal protection) was channelized until they no longer meet the scientific definitions of what a river even is. When I read written accounts of Davey Crockett regarding his adventures on West Tennessee rivers, I might as well be reading about dinosaurs. The river beds he traveled are now sandy dry gullies, and the wetlands he hunted were drained, cleared, and turned into row cropland. And all that destruction in the name of flood control has actually made flooding worse. The rivers were channelized, but now they just fill with sediment from erosion because the wetlands were destroyed. You can't cheat nature.

But the most tragic story in the tale of Tennessee rivers has to be the story of the Little Tennessee River, also called the Little T. Never heard of it? There is a reason. It is gone and buried. This tributary of the big Tennessee River was a pristine mountain stream surrounded by Cherokee village sites and the most fertile crop land in East Tennessee. It formed a deep gorge along the southern border of the Great Smoky Mountains National Park before winding through the rolling hills of the Tennessee Valley. In 1944, a 480 foot tall dam was built at Fontana Village, turning the gorge that the Little Tennessee roared through into a silent lake. In the proceeding decades there were three more dams built downstream, but there was still a little piece of the lower river left. In 1979, after the Supreme Court pro-dam ruling over the fate of the tiny endangered Snail Darter, TVA closed the gates of its 69th dam and turned the small remaining 35 mile stretch of the Little Tennessee into Tellico Lake. This flooded 16,000 acres and buried Chota, the historical site of the de-facto capital of the Cherokee Nation. By the way, it also flooded the historic site of the Cherokee Village, Tanasi, the namesake of Tennessee. In addition to the area flooded, TVA took 23,000 additional acres of farmland. This wasn't the Great Depression era anymore, and many of the farmers fought it. In the end they got an average of $600 per acre, sometimes lower. Then the developers got it. How much does a half acre lot go for now? About $750,000. But how much green energy does this boondoggle of a dam make you ask? None at all. It has no turbines. It simply diverts water into another reservoir. If there was one thing positive that came out of the demise of the Little Tennessee, was that it was the final martyr in the war to save many remaining rivers. The project had to be specially excluded from the Endangered Species Act, and there was not an appetite to try it again.

This was the very end of the dam building era. TVA cancelled their plans for a new Duck River dam they were going to build in the 1980's that would have destroyed vast swaths of Middle Tennessee. Thank God.

So needless to say, when trying to plan my great overnight canoe adventure, my pickings were slim. There was one river on my list left to research, the Elk River in southern Middle Tennessee. The Elk begins at the western foot of the Cumberland Plateau, in Grundy County, TN. It flows 195 miles, across the southernmost counties of Middle Tennessee, where it eventually crosses into Alabama and flows into Wheeler Lake on the Tennessee River. It's upper waters are dammed by the Elk River Dam on the Woods Reservoir, which was built to provide cooling water for the wind tunnels at the Tullahoma Air Force Base. It is dammed again by Tims Ford Dam to form Tims Ford Lake. After Tims Ford Dam, the Elk flows free until reaches the Tennessee River. Not very far after it crosses into Alabama, it becomes slack water for Wheeler Lake. But from Tims Ford to near the state line, about 100 miles, it actually flows like a river inside its actual natural riverbed. I had driven along the stretch from Winchester to Fayetteville many times, and it always seemed like a shallow, rocky stream, really perfect for canoeing. The same roadway was covered with billboard advertisements for canoe rentals in the area. A little internet research quickly discovered a couple of outfitters in Kelso, TN, that ran trips on the 45 mile stretch between Tims Ford and Fayetteville. This river was also located in a convenient place, about three hours for any West Tennessee folks and three or less hours for anyone from East Tennessee that I could talk into going. I called Elk River Canoe Rental in Kelso and was advised that the best 23 mile stretch was running the river from Tims Ford Dam to the rental base in Kelso. The other overnight option was to run from the base down to Fayetteville, about the same mileage. According to the outfitter, the best fishing was closer to the dam. We really wanted to incorporate fishing into this trip, and we needed all the luck we could get. We choose the portion nearer the dam.

Besides Jack and Rob, the roster for this trip ended up being my cousin John, who lives in Pikeville, and two of my friends from work, Kyle and Miles. Kyle and Miles were the only ones that had not been on a trip with me before so we spent a lot of time planning and plotting what everyone needed to bring. Canoe trips open up the Pandora's box of outdoor adventure planning. Because you are essentially not limited by the weight and size of your equipment, you can plan a plethora of activities. Of course you can fish, but you also can plan elaborate cookouts and camp set ups. I had a two hour conference call with Rob about equipment and the menu. Then there was a couple of rounds of highly instructional e-mails to the group to spell out our plan. Miles was far and above the biggest fisherman of the group. He was leading the trout fishing effort, doing research, and putting together a common tackle box. Trout fishing was a completely new pursuit for all of us so we really had no idea what we were getting into.

We planned and planned, but the time for the trip soon rolled around, in mid-April. It had been a cool spring, with lows down in the high 30's just a week before the trip. But my biggest worry was not the temperature, it was the rain. It had not been very wet, but there had been a few two to three day periods of rain that flooded up the rivers and creeks around home. An event like that would flood out our potential campsites and make fishing very difficult. I was relieved that when the week rolled around there were just some scattered storms rolling through the area on Thursday. Everything was supposed to clear out by the start of our trip on Friday morning.

The afternoon before we left, my cousin had to back out because of an emergency at work. Of course this took away our even number, meaning there would be a single paddler in one of the canoes. That is just something that happens on canoe trips no matter how hard you try to make sure you have an even number group. I left my house around 5:30 am. We rendezvoused a couple of times to consolidate vehicles. We then followed I-65 down to the Lewisburg exit and followed Highway 64 past Fayetteville. The Smithland Road turnoff was on the left side of the highway. The road was very narrow and wound into the steep hills covered in mixed woods and pastures. The Plateau had been visible on the eastern horizon, but was now quickly obscured as we descended deeper into the hollow that we hoped was leading us to the river. Rob had beat us there and had been walking around while giving us text updates. There was no one there, but they had left a note saying that they were checking river levels and would be back around 9:30. Soon we pulled into a clearing with a very rustic looking shop and an open shed full of life jackets and paddles. There were half a dozen vans parked in the field, all hooked up to trailers full of canoes and kayaks. There were more trailers of boats just sitting around in the weeds.

I called the number on the note. Dwight, whom I had spoken with before when making reservations, answered and said they were just a few minutes away. Soon a truck drove through the gate into the clearing. Dwight and Ben got out and introduced themselves. They told us to walk down the trail and take a look at the take out spot while they went inside and got the paper work. We walked down a trail for about a hundred yards through the woods until it came to a rickety wooden staircase that led down to a gravel beach by the river. There was a field on a hill by the beach and we saw a small camper parked there. The water was shallow and the current was moving fast towards a sharp bend to the right. We tried to memorize it the best we could. We would get one shot at this place tomorrow and didn't want screw up and run past it. We headed back up to the shop where Ben had our paperwork ready. We signed our waivers, paid $35 each in cash, and picked out our paddles and life jackets. Ben handed out some maps to us and went over a few waypoints. I made notes on my map the best I could, but his directions about Old Dam Road access were a little muddled. He talked about fishing regulations, "If you eat what you catch don't worry about it." And he talked about camping rules, "Stay on the beaches and bars and clean up your mess." It was simple enough. Because we had an odd number, he loaded one 15 foot canoe on the trailer for the single paddler, which would be theoretically easier to handle than the 18 foot canoes. We loaded our gear into the back of a ten passenger van which was already hooked up to a trailer. Ben was going to drive and was very impressed with the small amount of stuff we were bringing. We piled in the dusty seats and headed out.

The ride to the dam took about 30 minutes, and Ben kept us entertained with river stories. I was riding in the very back of the van and really couldn't see much regarding where were going until we pulled off the road onto the river access. From our take in point, I couldn't actually see the concrete portion of the dam and the spillway, but I could see the massive rock levy. Below it the river flowed very shallow over a wide stretch of rocks, until the channel deepened and the water calmed before it reached the long gravel beach that we were driving onto.

We parked on the beach and Ben unloaded our three canoes, placing them in the edge of the water, while we unloaded our gear. We had packed carefully. Besides our fishing gear, we had five backpacks and three coolers. That was it. On a canoe trip, if you aren't careful, the crap people carry can get out of control. There were two packs and a cooler in two canoes and one pack and one cooler in the single canoe, which I volunteered to take on first. Everything was loaded and we said good bye to Ben. It was 10:30 a.m. and past time to get going. I got a helpful push to get launched and was soon in the channel and headed downriver. It was still very overcast and there was a cool wind on the water. It felt good to have a paddle in my hands again.

With the more seasonal temperatures in the last two weeks, the world had finally turned green. The trees were not quite the "hurt your eyes" bright green of May and early June, and still had some yellows and browns in the canopy. The undergrowth had completely emerged in the last week and the briars, umbrella plants, and poison ivy were forming a thick carpet along the floor of the woods. I had even found a couple of ticks crawling on me the weekend before. Needless to say, I was going to be extra careful to not repeat another tick, chigger, and poison ivy fiasco like I had on the Obed hiking trip. I was wearing my synthetic hiking pants on top of running shorts that had a mesh liner. My shirt was my button up hiking shirt with the sleeves rolled up (but had the quick option to cover up more for bugs or brush). We were also all wearing water shoes, which were going to be a necessity on the rough rock bottom.

The other two canoes quickly overtook me, and we stayed close together for the first couple of turns in the river. We got near a decent size gravel beach, and Miles thought it would be a good first place to try to fish. We paddled fast out of the current and beached our canoes on a long strip of gravel below a short embankment. Most of the river was only about two feet deep and there were large rocks in the middle of the current. Miles got out his tackle box and realized that the nightcrawlers and kernel corn had been left in the bed of his truck. Fortunately, we still had plenty of bass stuff, some of which we hoped would be effective on trout. I ended up choosing a grub with a spinner to try. Rob had a simple casting spoon. Most of the group worked downstream along the beach. Rob started to work the current right in front of us, and I was heavily eyeing two logs upstream along the bank, which formed a v shape in front of a deep pool. I waded into the edge of the water and casted a couple of times. The current was much stronger than I had anticipated, and it ripped the little spinner downstream quickly. I began to realize that working the lure in this water was going to depend on playing the current more than actually using the reel. I also realized the that water was ridiculously cold. It was not quite Smoky Mountain stream in winter cold, but it was pretty close. My feet began to ache from the blood being forced out within ten or fifteen seconds. I didn't see myself spending much time in the water.

I tried to reach the pool by the logs, first climbing up the small embankment. Of course it was completely covered with poison ivy. I was glad that I had not attempted to zip off the legs of my pants. Toward the end of the embankment I found myself directly over the deep pool. On the second cast I hung the lure under one of the logs. The pool was way too deep to attempt to wade through, so I had to break the line. I then picked my way carefully through the poison ivy and back to my tackle box that I had left on the beach, ending my first lesson of what not to do.

I tied another spinner on, identical to the first one, and set out again. In a short conversation with Miles, he was thinking that we needed to find a spot with some deeper pools. There was just too much fast shallow water here. This time I worked my way out to the middle of the river and tried to cast in the shallows on the opposite bank. It was just too cold to stand there for long. The bottom was rock and grass it was really easy to hold your footing as long as the current was not too strong. After a few casts I started to wade upstream to try to get above the logs and pool. I made it on to bar of muddy gravel and let my feet thaw for a minute. I started to cast above the logs. Rob was in the shallows, in the main current where I had been, but closer to the log pool. He was casting right into the open end of the "v". I was trying to not lose my lure again when I heard him yell and laugh. I looked up and he was reeling in a rainbow trout. It was small, but still a keeper. Miles came down and helped him get it on the stinger. Well, at least we knew we would have a little of nature's bounty for dinner that night.

I continued to fish the head of the pool. Rob went back to his hole again. I wandered up the bank for a piece, and I found a nice folding knife lying on the gravel just inches from the water. There was no rust on it so it had not been lost very long. I closed it and put it in my back pocket, happy that this stop yielded some luck for me, even if it was a knife and not a fish. When I turned around to look down stream again, Rob was pulling another trout out of that hole. I worked my way back onto the bank and tried to cast directly down into the pool again. Again, I got nothing until I eventually hung the spinner under the same log again. I worked my way through the poison ivy and back to the beach. Rob pulled another trout out of his hole. I decided to give up on that pool and picked out a small reflective minnow lure, thinking that it was the closest thing I could find that looked like Rob's lucky spoon. It started to thunder to the south of us, and the overcast sky got darker. I casted the new lure out in the current a few times but it was too shallow and swift there for much of a chance. By this time the rest of the group had pretty much given up and gathered around the boats. Rob got a few more cast in on his hole before we decided to move on down the river. By the time we got back into the channel a light rain started to fall.

The rain didn't last long, and I was barely even tempted to dig my jacket out of my pack. I was ahead of the group for several bends in the river. There were a few places where it got narrow, and the current was really ripping along the shallows. I realized that paddling single was going to give me a big advantage in shallow water. Other than that, it really sucked, especially when you weren't near anyone to talk to. I wasn't by myself for long though. The river widened back out the others caught up. Miles and Kyle got in front as we neared another gravel beach, this one much longer than the first. It extended far down to the next bend in the river. There was a turkey gobbling off on the bank above us. I over shot where they landed and ended up about thirty yards further down. Miles had it in his mind to climb up the bank and see if he could find the turkey. His plan ended when he saw a copperhead laid out on a flat rock above where he was about to step. I missed all of this because I was further away and trying to get my rod ready. Rob and Jack beached beside Kyle and Miles and they started to fish there. Kyle and Miles walked further down the beach to the next bend, out of sight.

I spotted a deeper hole upstream from a couple of logs on the opposite bank so I decided to wade over to it. The water was still very cold, but bearable now for long periods of time. The distance from the dam made it just a little warmer. It was no deeper than knee deep at least until the far bank. I did a few shorter casts just to watch the action of the minnow. It stayed about 3 or 4 inches below the surface and swam perfectly as long as it was against the current. As I moved on closer to the hole on the opposite bank I felt a tug on my sleeve. Rob's lure had hooked the sleeve of my shirt. I have no idea how in the world he threw it that far but he did. It must have been twenty yards. "I caught three trout and a

Bill!!", he said. It was pretty funny, but I made sure I kept further away from him.

I fished that hole with no luck until a tangle in my line made me go back to the bank to cut it out. While I was working on it, Rob caught another nice keeper and we got it on the stringer, which was tied on to the back of Miles's canoe. I waded back out to work that snag area, but again, no luck. It started to thunder more, still to the south of us. I saw Kyle walking by himself along the beach toward us. He wasn't carrying a fish. We started to gather back around the canoes, knowing that it was about time to get back on the water. It was almost 2:00 p.m., and I didn't know if we had made it much more than a mile down river. We had a long way to go. Kyle told us that Miles had found a hole and had caught several small ones that he had thrown back. He didn't want to leave it yet so we were supposed to pick him up on the way. We loaded up the canoes and set off again. As we rounded the bend, Miles was wading on the inside shore. His line was hung up under a log. I tried to grab it when I went by, but I was going too fast and the line snapped. Kyle picked up Miles, and we all started down the river with the goal of putting some real distance behind us.

The river widened, the current slowed, and I quickly fell behind the pack. Another light shower fell for a minute and subsided. I was hopeful things would improve because I knew the whole weather system was supposed to be moving out of the area, and we were generally moving west at the same time. The other two canoes got pretty far out ahead, and after a while I could only catch a glimpse of them at the far edge of a bend. I could occasionally hear voices traveling back up to me along the water. Most stretches of the river had a high bluff on one side and a shorter bank on the opposing side which usually contained some type of farmland, either row crop or pasture. The bluff sides were typically 30 to 50 feet high, with very little exposed rock. They were usually just a steep embankment of undergrowth capped with a few boulders, tall oaks, and hickories. Usually the banks consisted of gravel bars, no more than 3 or 4 feet above the water, but sometimes they were composed of sheer slabs of rock that extended down below the water. Every long stretch of river seemed to contain at least one island between the bends. The islands varied greatly in shape, length, and height. Some were just shallow gravel bars scattered with weeds and saplings. Some were 5 or 6 feet above the water, over 50 yards long, and covered in old growth timber. Despite the presence of farmland, I hardly ever saw a house, even from a distance. There were a handful of cabins on the bluff tops, most appeared unoccupied. Occasionally by the water there would be a small covered deck with a porch swing or a couple of benches, usually long abandoned and half swallowed by the undergrowth. Every mile or so we saw a "Posted" sign, typically where a creek fed into the river, but these were several dozen yards away from the water and would not have impeded camping on the bank.

Ben had mentioned the Elk is listed as one of the cleanest rivers in the state and even after a few miles I quickly agreed with that assessment. Other than an occasional faded beer can or small piece of agriculture trash caught in a log jam, we essentially saw no pollution along the 23 mile stretch of river. For a river in the Southeast, completely bounded by private land, that is highly unusual. My family owns land that borders the Forked Deer River in Madison County, and I honestly believe there are places in the river bottom where the forest floor contains more garbage than it does fallen leaves. But on the Elk, if it wasn't for the presence of farmland, it would have been easy to believe that it was managed by the National Park Service. I think this cleanliness is primarily due to the lack of population density and partly due to the TWRA officer presence involved with Tim's Ford Lake. Whatever the cause, I am grateful to see the effect.

We would occasionally pass fly fisherman wading in the current or a group of fishing kayaks. These people were obviously accessing the river someway, but I couldn't decipher how with my map, which seemed more useless by the hour. There were so many bends, turns, islands, and creeks that I could not match where we were or where we were going. I should have used my compass more, but I was keeping it in the top of my pack with the rest of the maps, and it was hard to get to. The only true waypoints were the bridges, which Ben had pointed out on our maps at the outfitter. There was a farm bridge at mile 6, a real concrete bridge called Ferris Creek Road at mile 9. There was some type of access at Dam Ford Road around mile 14. Shiloh bridge, or Champ Road, was at mile 21. It was getting on 3:00 p.m. now and we had not spotted a single one of these, which was making me nervous. I was pretty far behind now, only catching glimpses of the others at the end of a long straight stretch. We finally went under the farm bridge. Somebody had put a lot of work into it a long time ago, but today it looks like it is a couple of bad floods away from collapsing. We came along on some fishing kayaks. I saw Rob and Jack talking to them. Not far later, they had stopped in the middle of the river and waited for me to catch up. I said we needed to have a conference.

We all beached along a very wide gravel bar at the mouth of creek. The current was very strong through the narrow channel that remained. I pulled my maps out and walked over to the others to try to figure out where we were. Jack told me what the kayak folks had said. We were a little more than 6 miles in at this point. Looking at the map and the clock, our prospects were not looking good. I had wanted to make around mile 14 to make camp, in order for us have an easy second day with time to eat a good victory meal. To make that mark would have meant that we would have had to paddle until dark and maybe longer. Looking at the map, there seemed to be a possible shortcut. If we could make past the Ferris Creek Bridge before we camped, we could have a short few miles in the morning, put out at Dam Ford Road, call Ben, and have him come pick us up. Assuming it worked, it would shave about 10 miles off the whole trip.

The plan was accepted and now with a renewed sense of hope, we had a snack and fished. Most of the group was spreading out into the swift current and downstream. I walked up to the head of the beach were the water was deeper and calmer. After 10 or 15 minutes with no bites, I decided to try the downstream end. Of course Rob was wearing them out in the swift part of the narrow channel. He was catching mainly small ones, but at some point he caught a Brown trout that was at least 15 inches. It was a beautiful looking fish with large spots along its greenish brown and silver sides.

Of course, some purist fisherman deride tailwater stocked trout (trout stocked in cold water under dams) because they don't "naturally live there". That is just bull crap snobbery. If you are truly looking for only "native fish", good luck. I mentioned earlier how in the twentieth century people couldn't help damming every river they saw. In the eighteenth and nineteenth century people couldn't help carrying fish eggs and minnows with them every time they got on a boat. I am not kidding. European fish are in America. American fish are all over the world. The beautiful Brown trout, is originally from northern Europe. The Rainbow is from the Pacific tributaries of North America. The Large Mouth bass and the Channel catfish are native to Tennessee. The same Channel catfish are in Malaysia. Do you know where the world record Large Mouth bass was caught? A very long way from the Southeast; in Lake Biwa, Japan.

I moved back to the strong current, just down from where Rob was. On my second cast I felt a strike and began to reel it in quick. The trout broke the surface a couple of times, and when I got him in close I saw he was pretty small Rainbow. I picked him up and worked the treble hook out with the small pliers I kept in my breast pocket. He was soft and smooth, not like any fish I had ever held before. After I got the hook out I gently lowered him back in the shallow, grassy water by the bank. My attention turned back downstream where Rob was. He had hung the lucky spoon in a tree. Not just any tree, but an oak that was overhanging the river at a 45 degree angle. The line led to a branch that was at least 25 feet over the water. I thought the lucky spoon was sunk for sure.

Miles went down to help him and they tried to work the line back and forth. At one point Rob worked over to the bank and started to climb up the tree. I thought he was nuts. It was a $3 lure, but it was really was lucky. He got halfway up and logic prevailed. After he got back in the water they kept at it and somehow, someway, it freed itself and fell into the river. I couldn't believe it.

We had the lucky spoon back, but there wasn't much time to fish. It was getting near time to get back on the river. The thunder seemed to have finally left us, and the sky was clearing with the wind dying down. I subtly asked for volunteers to take my spot in the single canoe. Kyle jumped in and I got his spot in front of Miles. Kyle got the boat in the water first and took a quick lead, moving a lot faster than I had been over the last 6 or 7 miles. I enjoyed the conversation and ability to take a five second rest without losing momentum. We were all moving quick now and finally reached the Ferris Creek bridge. It was a pretty high bridge, but there was some kind of access trail under the road bed were you could have put in or taken out.

It was getting on near 5:00 p.m. now and we started to look for a campsite. The sun was going to set at 7:30 p.m. and we had a lot of camp chores ahead of us. From looking at the thickness of the undergrowth, it was apparent that we were going to camp on a gravel bar. I would rather face the possibility of getting flooded out in the night versus sleeping in the middle of a tick filled poison ivy patch. We were not really seeing any gravel bars that were level enough or wide enough to hold three tents and had space to cook.

The whole group was soon gathered back up at very shallow and swift moving section beside a low lying island. We had to jump out and drag the canoes for a dozen yards or so before reaching deeper water on the other side of a large log jam. I mentioned just camping there, but the point was brought up that the gravel bar was incredibly low. The event of a water release from the dam was unlikely, but it probably was a good idea to give the river a couple of feet of leeway. Our group stayed together and slowly paddled for the next few bends, scanning the banks closely. On a straight stretch we came upon an elevated gravel beach on the left bank which stretched for a good 50 yards and was 10 yards wide at some points. It was bisected by a washed out creek bed mouth which fed into some murky water standing in the eddies of snags lining the steep bank. We landed first on the part of the beach upstream from the creek bed and explored a wide, washed out drainage that led into the woods. The first part of the beach was narrow. We entertained camping in the drainage until we encountered deep mud. As we stood on the beach trying to figure out how to set up camp we noticed that the second part of the gravel beach was much longer, flatter, and wider. Its highest point was a good four feet above the water level. We pushed off into the river again, landed on the lowest angle slope of the beach, and walked the area. There was plenty of room for tents at the far end of the beach were the gravel was smaller and the grade was almost flat. There was an area with larger rocks that looked like a good place to build a fire and cook. There were no decent holes in the immediate current for fishing, but it was 5:30 p.m. and there was no time to get picky.

The tents were unloaded, set up, and filled with sleeping pads and bags. I started to work on the fire while most of the others gathered drift wood from the drainage area. I brought one of my newest toys, a tactical tomahawk, and it got used for firewood chopping and tent stake hammering. I always like to see my impulse Amazon purchases put to actual use. The firewood crew also had Miles' machete. Rob used my collapsible shovel to dig a pit for cooking with the grill top we had brought. He dug the hold slightly larger than the grill, arranged four larger rocks to act as support on the edges, and scooped the gravel away from one end to allow more air to reach the coals. I got the fire going relatively easily, and by the time I turned my attention away from it there was enough firewood piled beside me to last two nights. Many aspects of traveling with a larger number of people make processes slower in general, except in the area of firewood collection. It would have taken two people over an hour to collect that much.

We got the fire established with large chunks of wood that would eventually produce our cooking coals. It was 6:30 p.m. now and there was plenty to do in the meantime. There was a stringer of seven fish to clean, and I needed to get started cooking the sides for the dinner. I got my MSR stove and Rob's JetBoil set up on some flat ground where the canoes were beached. Before I started cooking I wanted to see how the fish preparation was going. Miles tried to filet one of the smaller trout but they were just too small. He decided it was best just to skin them, clean them, and cook them whole, tail still attached. We made individual aluminum foil sheets for each fish. After Miles cleaned each one, they were season with salt, pepper, garlic powder, red pepper, and lemon juice, then sealed in an aluminum pouch. There was still a lot for me to do so I left the biology class and went back to my makeshift kitchen. I got the potatoes going and started on the mac n cheese. It was almost dark now and the sun had dipped below the trees.

The coals had finally built up in the fire, and Rob shoveled some into the cooking pit and started to get ready to grill. He had packed the rib eyes in freezer bags full of marinade, six steaks in all, two to a bag. The grill top wasn't very big so he started with two steaks, turning them with tongs. It was headlamp time and we all turned on our lights, with a couple of us huddling over the cooking to give him some extra light. At this point we encountered a significant safety hazard involved with the pit cooking experiment. The rocks in the damp earth that we had dug into had begun to get so hot that the moisture in them was boiling quickly, causing pressure to build in the small porous spaces until they exploded. This sent hot, razor sharp, shards of rock flying out of the pit. Rob and I were both hit in the face, and we quickly learned to keep our distance. Rob has some refined grilling skills and was undeterred by the darkness and flying shrapnel, cooking both steaks to a perfect medium. We put them on plates, passed them along, and put the remaining four on the grill top. We still kept our distance but the rocks were not popping as much now. The last batch was done soon. We spilt the sixth steak between us. Grabbing fresh beers and helping ourselves to the sides in the pots, we all sat around the fire and ate. It was best dinner I had ever eaten on the trail.

As full as we were, we were determined not to stop yet. There was still the bounty of our fishing efforts. We shoveled more coals into the pit and placed the foil wrapped fish on the grill. In less than 10 minutes the trout were starting to finish cooking, and Miles passed them out as they were done. The bones were almost like course hairs, but we raked the meat down the sides with our forks and enjoyed every bite. I was impressed how mild of tasting fish it was. We were even more full now, but of course there is always room for sausage. I put the pound of kielbasa I brought on the grill, and it was ready in about five minutes. After we shared it we were finally done with dinner, except we then had to pass around Jack's peanut butter cookies as a desert course. It was getting on 9:00 p.m. by the time we actually stopped eating and settled into the typical campfire routine. Around 11:00 p.m., the group started to dwindle down and head off to the tents. The night had turned cool. My new air pad was very comfortable, and I fell asleep quick.

It is always a gamble to sleep without the rain fly, but the night was clear and I thought it was worth the risk. I woke to the sound of the birds and the river rushing along the bank. The dawn sky was clear, and the sun was rising over the water almost directly up river, turning the light morning fog on the water into a shimmering white mist. It was going to be a nice spring day.

Rob was walking down the bank with his filter. Everyone else was up and moving by now so I realized I needed to finally get going. I as I walked over to the canoes to gather water bottles, Miles and Kyle were standing down on the bank fishing. The temperature was cool, but I was ok with just rolling the sleeves down on my shirt. I followed Rob across the creek to the head of the beach were the water was running clearer. We filled up a few bottles and got back to camp to get breakfast started. We found out at some point in the morning Rob's lucky spoon had been lost under a log on the far bank. Oh well, we weren't planning on much fishing on the way out anyway.

The stoves were set up on the cooler tops. Coffee was started and the first batch of bacon got going. Out of the three skillet fulls of bacon we cooked, only one got knocked onto the ground and some of it got saved anyway. Then Rob got started on his egg masterpiece. Butter, peppers, onions, and cheese were added in. The eggs had been pre-wisked and transported in two large water bottles in Rob's cooler. He made two batches, and it was passed around along with the plate full of bacon. The trend for the trip continued. It was the best breakfast I have ever had on the trail.

We broke down camp quick and the boats were loaded by 8:45 a.m., which I thought was impressive. It was warming up quick now. The sunny morning was already warmer than mid-day had been the day before. I took off my button up and stuffed it in my pack, just wearing my running t-shirt. Kyle said he was fine going by himself again. I switched my pack into the canoe with Miles, then we were on our way. In retrospect, we really should have dumped the canoes out before we re-loaded them. There was a lot of water sloshing around in the bottom. Every time someone jumped in from standing in the water, a little bit of river got brought in from shoes and pants legs. Over time it really started to add up and pretty much anything that sat in the bottom of the canoe for any amount of time was getting soaked, especially the bottom of our packs. At some point I realized that anything that I had not waterproofed in my pack had gotten wet, just from the water sloshing around in the canoe and splashing from the paddles. Any map or piece of paper in my pocket that was not in a plastic bag, got completely soaked from the paddle dripping each time I changed sides. It was a canoeing lesson that I forgotten but quickly relearned.

Now back in the current and thinking we only had about 4 or so miles to go, spirits were high. We were moving quick in the narrow parts of the river, which seemed more frequent. Kyle got ahead and stayed in front for quite a way. There were a few decent places to camp after our beach, but I was glad we had chosen to camp where we did. Soon the banks of the river became steeper and the woods became thicker. There were very large islands, but they were way too thick with undergrowth to provide a place to camp.

Soon it was a little after 10:00 a.m. and I was really thinking that Old Dam Road had to be getting close. We had passed Beans Creek on our left (the largest tributary stream we encountered), and I was expecting to see the road access after every turn. Ben had tried to explain to us how to spot it by seeing a flag that may or may not have been washed away. I didn't understand how it could have been so hard to see, but never the less, I was not seeing it. The map was no help. On the Google map it looked like the road continued on the south bank of the river. The map that Ben had given us showed the road only on the north bank. The Google map showed a straight stretch of open river perpendicular to the ford access. So when we reached a large shallow island stretching for a couple hundred yards with fast moving currents to the left and right, I thought nothing of it. The left looked wider and clearer. The right looked narrow, with more waves and log jams. Kyle started leading to the left, and we followed him. Rob and Jack headed right. As we were splitting I looked down the right side and saw limestone rocks piled on the bank, and what looked like a truck and people through the trees. I yelled toward Jack and Rob while pointing, "Is that a road?" Through the rushing roar of the river, I could not hear them say anything, and I was not sure that they heard me. It was too late to do anything about it anyway now. As the trees separating us sped by, I could catch glimpses of the other canoe, but I could not see much. We had to concentrate on steering ourselves through the rocks and logs. When we joined back up with them at the end of the island, they had not gotten any useful information from the man on the bank. He didn't know the name of the road, where we was, or how he got there. Typical local directions.

I had a bad feeling about the whole thing, especially the way that those limestone rocks, which did not belong on the bank, were piled along the edge of the water. But the map showed no trace of that gigantic island, and it really didn't seem like a place for a "ford". Either way, we were going down river now.

The river wound and wound, but the further we went without seeing any sign of a road, the more I began to think we were making the rest of the planned trip whether we wanted to or not. We reached a bend with a wooded bluff on the right that was higher than any other I had seen. After the bluff the banks remained steep. We soon ran into a group of kayak fisherman, the first large group of the day. Miles and I were first in the line and paddled in close to ask directions. The main one that talked was an older man with short gray hair. After we told them where were we were headed, the highlights of the conversation included, "Old Dam road was behind us", "Elk River Canoe was a good days float and it would take all the remaining daylight to get there", "They would see us around dark", "The only other place to take out is Shiloh bridge, but that will take a very long time too, probably close to dark". The words were demoralizing by themselves, but I was more upset that the rest of my group heard him. It wasn't demoralizing for me because I didn't believe a word that old man said. First, we were a good mile past the missed Old Dam Road, which was mile 14, so we were now around 9 miles from the vehicles. It was a little after 10:00 a.m., so we had gone five miles in about an hour and fifteen minutes. At the pace were going, I figured we had around two and a half hours of paddling left. Second, I noticed the old man's companions were laughing while he was talking to us, which didn't aid in the veracity of the information they were giving. I thought we were going to be fine, but the decision was made to try for the Shiloh Bridge takeout if possible. I was fine with it, but whether or not you believed my map or the local yokels, we still had a good ways to go.

At this point in the trip, we really went into auto pilot mode. Miles and I got out front and kept the lead for a long time. We kept a good pace and were only slowed down during a long stretch going north against a strong head wind. The sky was clear, and the sun was getting high and hot. Having to jump out occasionally to drag the canoe across shallow rocks was a relief to cool off. At one point in the long stretch, Miles pointed out a bald eagle as it swooped over us. I have not seen one in the wild since I was on an elementary field trip to Reelfoot Lake. I could only see it from the back and caught just a glimpse of its white head. It was huge and covered the width of the river in one flap of its wings, passing over us twice and disappearing into the trees again. What a magnificent creature. The day had not gone great since breakfast, but our eagle visit seemed to get things back on the right track.

We rounded a sharp bend and started back south. I got out my soaked map and carefully unfolded it. The bend we were on was either not that far away from the stretch were we saw the yokels, or very close to the Shiloh Bridge. It was getting on near noon. I was wanting to stop to eat and re-group soon, but we couldn't find a decent spot so we pressed on. After a slight turn in the river we spotted a bridge. To the right there was a ramp where kayaks were being unloaded from a van parked on a steep bank about twenty feet above the water. This had to be the spot that we had been told about. We quit paddling and drifted down to the ramp. The van that was unloading was from Elk River Canoe.

I yelled up the driver, "You from Elk River Canoe?"

"Yeah", he shouted down.

"Can you give us a ride back?"

"Well, I guess. But can you paddle two more miles?"

I would have paid a hundred dollars to have had the chance to flip that old man yokel into the river. I told the Elk River guy about what we had been told, and he described the old man. Apparently he gets enjoyment out of trying to discourage people and ruin their trips. Anyway, the rest of the group caught up, and I gave them the good news. We paddled under the bridge and got slowed down trying to dodge all the yahoos that had just put in. It was really awful to be that close to that many loud people after being out by ourselves for so long. They had water guns. They had radios. They zig zagged across the river with no idea of what they were doing. We had to wait in line to get through narrow spots. After a half a mile or so we got past them and pushed on hard. Soon we got to the large clear cuts that Dwight had told us would be a sign that the shop was getting close. The high hills and bluffs were scarred up with bare spots and thick undergrowth, and the water was murky from erosion. I was glad to be nearing the end of the trip. I was sure Kyle was too, considering that he had paddled nearly 14 miles by himself. We were all grouped up again when we turned a bend and saw the long rock beach with the staircase and the campground on the hill. It was a little after 12:30 p.m. when we beached our canoes and started to unload, which was the exact time I thought we would finish. Despite our two failed attempts to cut our trip short, it felt good to accomplish the whole 23 mile stretch.

Dwight was down on the beach and helped us carry all the gear up to the parking lot, which had about fifty cars in it now. We loaded the truck, changed into dry clothes, and had a good victory lunch at Buffalo Wild Wings in Fayetteville.

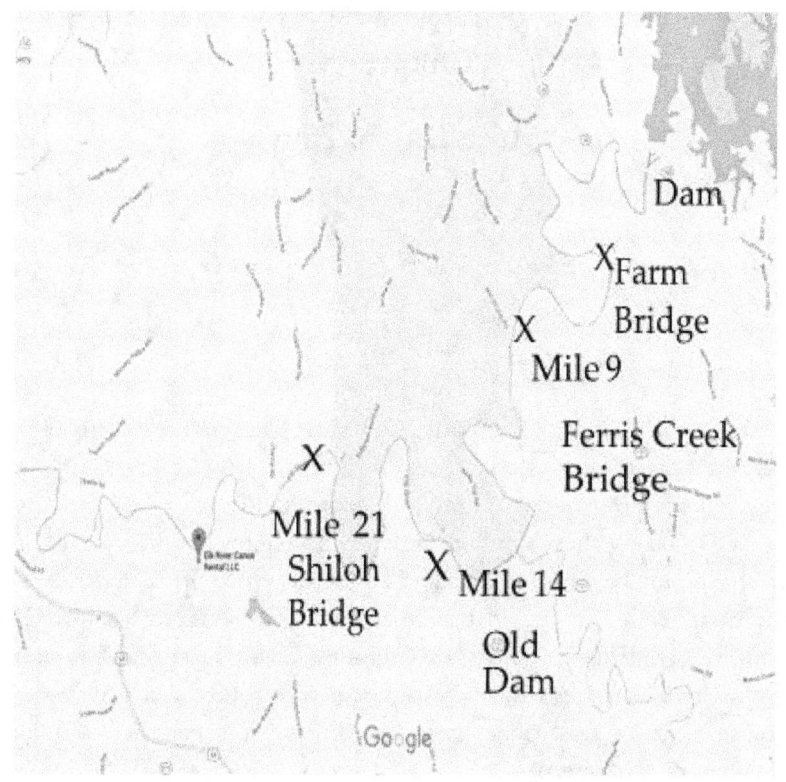

Chapter X

More Day to Dawn

"Only that day dawns to which we are awake. There is more day to dawn, The sun is but a morning star"

-*Henry David Thoreau, Walden*

There is a lot more to explore. Of course, I never meant this book to cover everything worth looking at on the entirety of the Cumberland Plateau. I am not even sure how long that would even take. Honestly, I have been making these types of trips to the region for the past 14 years, and I have only begun to understand all that it has to offer. There are still many State Parks on the Plateau that I have not visited, such as Rock Island, Burgess Falls, Edgar Evins, Cummins Falls, Cumberland Mountain, Pickett, Cove Lake, and Indian Mountain. Of course I also want to see more of Frozen Head on a day when I have less concern over losing extremities to frostbite.

Then, there are the State Natural Areas, like Bone Cave, Walls of Jericho, and Virgin Falls. Straddling the state line with Kentucky is the Big South Fork National River and Recreation Area, which ultimately connects to the 2.1 million acre Daniel Boone National Forest. Then there are the historical parks such as the Birthplace of Alvin York, the birthplace of Cordell Hull, the Civil War battlefield site of Lookout Mountain, Cumberland Gap National Historical Park, and the Moccasin Bend National Archeological District. And of course there are the private parks of Ruby Falls and Rock City.

As far as future river trips go, I think the Sequatchie River has a lot of potential. It has 116 miles of free flowing water that drains the entire Sequatchie Valley and not a single dam. My only problem with planning a multi-day trip was finding an outfitter that offered them. Of course, the same problem persists with the Obed River as well. I just need to find a person with a couple of river canoes that both would not mind letting me borrow them and would not be terribly upset if they never saw them again.

As far as the Cumberland Trail goes, there are 11 of the 14 segments that I have not even touched, and more trail is getting built each year. Even though the situation with Fiery Gizzard can be frustrating, I think in the end the park will be better once it is entirely (or almost entirely) contained on protected land. I really look forward to going back there soon to see the progress that been made through the dedicated work of the volunteers. Of course if I totally run out of trails, parks, and rivers on the Plateau, I can always tryout one of the 9,600 caves. I might look a little silly though carrying five headlamps, 50 batteries, and a dragging a few thousand yards of parachute cord behind me to mark my way back.

I hope have provided some direction and inspiration for people to get out there and enjoy, as well as protect, an often overlooked region that is readily accessible to anyone with the desire to venture outside. And remember, no matter what some trail guide, like this one, or some random stranger tells you, the level of difficulty is a very subjective matter. Even when the going gets hard, the woods are no place for discouragement. Just keep putting one foot in front of the other, look around, and I guarantee that you will see some pretty cool stuff. I know I have.

Notes and Sources

Before I attempted to write this book I thought I had a pretty good handle on the details of the Cumberland Plateau, but I really had no true appreciation for its history and the conservation efforts surrounding it. I have described my sources below. I would encourage everyone to do some further reading before their next trip, it will definitely enrich the experience. At minimum, get a good map to carry.

And if you are ever wanting to find some new ideas for adventures, you can check out my blog at:

http://bullmoosestrenuouslife.blogspot.com/

Or my Twitter:

https://twitter.com/billparnell25

Chapter I

Let me re-iterate the profound influence that the writings of John Muir have had on my pursuit of these attempts at adventures as well as my philosophies regarding our place in nature. If you were mildly entertained by this book, please take the time to read some real books written by someone who actually knew what they were doing.

Muir, John (1916). *A Thousand-Mile Walk to the Gulf.* **New York. Houghton Mifflin Company**

Muir, John (1915). *Travels in Alaska.* **Boston. Houghton Mifflin Company**

Regarding Civil War history, this is the link to the actual 1863 article in the New York times regarding Bragg's retreat from Tullahoma.

http://www.nytimes.com/1863/07/04/news/bragg-s-retreat-from-tullahoma.html

This article is about someone paddling the same route taken by John Donelson.

Bliss, Jessica (2016, November). "Nashville adventurer retraces John Donelson's historic river journey". *The Tennessean.* **Retrieved from www.Tennessean.com**

There is always good information about the history and the details of the Cumberland Plateau available from the National Park Service website.

https://www.nps.gov/biso/planyourvisit/upload/webgeo.pdf

These sites provided some of the geological ages of the sites I discussed. Geology, like every other science, has many issues that are far from settled, so there will be other age estimations out there. I am not a geologist so I just chose ones that seemed in the middle of the road.

http://portal.ncdenr.org/web/apnep/geology

https://www.sciencedaily.com/releases/2006/11/061117123212.htm

https://www.nps.gov/grsm/learn/nature/geology.htm#10/35.6238/-83.5757

https://www.nps.gov/mora/faqs.htm

Chapter II Frozen Head

The map in the chapter is from the free online version of the trail map. You can buy a nice map inside the Ranger Station at the main entrance on the right.

This is the Tennessee State Park website with park details and maps.

http://tnstateparks.com/assets/pdf/additional-content/park-maps/frozen-head_park-map.pdf

You can read many articles on the Barkley Marathons, but here is one of the more recent.

Dalek, Brian (2016, April). "The Barkley Marathons: One Person Finishes!", *Runner's World.* **Retrieved from www.runnersworld.com**

Chapter III Obed River

All current information about the Cumberland Trail project can be found on the Cumberland Trail Conference website. Maps are also provided for each segment of the trail and updates are given on the progress of construction.

http://cumberlandtrail.org/

If you are interested in the history and on-going struggle for the conservation of one of the great last unspoiled rivers in the South, check out the work of Tennessee Citizens for Wilderness Planning

http://tcwp.org/

Chapter IV Grassy Cove

The map came from the segment descriptions on the Cumberland Trails Conference website.

http://cumberlandtrail.org/

These are good articles about the cave systems on the Plateau, especially regarding the recent discovery of cave art.

Eilperin, J. (2004, November), "Tennessee Cave offers Trove of Undiscovered Creatures", *Washington Post,* Retrieved from http://www.washingtonpost.com

Ghianni, T. (2013, June), "Professor who found oldest US cave art says that there's more", www.reuters.com

Soslow, R. (2012, September), "Getting Lost in the Caves of Tennessee", *Washington Post,* Retrieved from http://www.washingtonpost.com

Chapter V Fall Creek Falls

As always there is good general information about the park at **www.tnstateparks.com**. However the map on that website is only of the short trails and overlooks around the visitor center. The map I included in the chapter was found on the Friends of Fall Creek Falls State Park website: **http://fallcreekfalls.org/maps.html**

Other information about the recent developments with the park:

Benton, B. (2013, July), "Fall Creek Falls Cabins Target of $1.4 Million Facelift", *Times Free Press,* Retrieved from www.timesfreepress.com

Rainwater, K. (2015, March), "Fall Creek Falls State Park Compete for 10 Best Honors", *Times Free Press,* Retrieved from www.timesfreepress.com

Chapter VI Savage Gulf and Stone Door

Before going on a trip to South Cumberland (including Fiery Gizzard), be sure to check the The Friends of South Cumberland website.

http://www.friendsofsouthcumberland.org

The map exerts in the chapter came from older map images on the internet, but good topographical maps are available at the ranger stations or through the Friends of South Cumberland site.

There are many governmental entities, such as the USDA, as well as conservation organizations such as the Arbor Day Foundation, that can provide an abundant amount of information on trees.

http://www.usda.gov/oce/climate_change/hubs/SoutheastFactSheet.pdf

http://www.seesouthernforests.org/discover-southern-forests/history/pre-1630

https://www.arborday.org/trees/treeguide

Chapter VII Fiery Gizzard

The Fiery Gizzard map exert was taken from the route update on the Friends of South Cumberland website. This is an actively changing park, so definitely visit the Friends site before your hike.

For information about the ongoing conservation efforts, The Land Trust for Tennessee homepage is a good start as well.

http://landtrusttn.org/

As well as The Conservation Fund.

http://www.conservationfund.org/projects/fiery-gizzard-trail

And Chattanooga's Times Free Press, is always a good source.

Sohn, P. (2010, September), "$4 Million Will Help Save Fiery Gizzard". *Times Free Press.* **Retrieved from www.timesfreepress.com**

Benton, B. (2016, March), "Another Landowner Asks Officials to Move the Fiery Gizzard Trial Off His Property". *Times Free Press.* **Retrieved from www.timesfreepress.com**

Chapter VIII Tennessee Gorge

This map for this section of the Cumberland Trail can be located with all the other section maps.

http://cumberlandtrail.org

The ABC affiliate for Chattanooga ran this piece in 2015:

"The History of Protecting the Tennessee River Gorge". *NewsChannel9.* **Retrieved from http://newschannel9.com/sponsored/hearts-for-humanity/the-history-of-protecting-the-tennessee-river-gorge**

For information about the history and conservation efforts for the Tennessee River, see the website of the Tennessee Riverkeeper organization.

http://www.tennesseeriver.org/riverhistory.html

Or of course the Tennessee River Gorge Trust website:

http://www.trgt.org

Chapter IX Elk River

The map is a modified Google Map of my creation. You are just going to have to believe me. It is either me or that crazy old man that will say that you are halfway to Mexico.

If you want to get really sad and upset, read this book about the rivers from my neck of the woods in West Tennessee.

Johnson, J. (2007). *Rivers Under Siege: The Troubled Saga of West Tennessee Wetlands.* **University of Tennessee Press.**

These are articles about Tellico Dam. People tend to forget as time goes along. The only reason why I even knew to start digging around about the Little Tennessee is because I remember reading a story about Fontana Village in a book about hiking in the Smokies that I read 20 years ago.

Wilson, R. (2008, April). "Tellico Dam Still Generating Debate". *Knoxville News Sentinel.* **Retrieved from http://archive.knoxnews.com/business/tellico-dam-still-generating-debate-ep-411807529-359923851.html**

Rawls, W. (1979, November). "Forgotten People of the Tellico Dam Fight". *The New York Times.* **Retrieved from http://www.nytimes.com/1979/11/11/archives/forgotten-people-of-the-tellico-dam-fight-right-of-eminent-domain.html?_r=1**

Special to The New York Times (1979, November). "Tellico Dam's Foes Lose Another Battle in Court". *The New York Times.* **Retrieved from http://www.nytimes.com/1979/11/10/archives/tellico-dams-foes-lose-another-battle-in-court**

www.ingramcontent.com/pod-product-compliance
Lightning Source LLC
Chambersburg PA
CBHW072142280526
45788CB00002B/742